Arsène & Arsenal

To Monty Fisher, Jeffrey Freeman, Mel Goldberg, Gary Mitchell, Steve Mono, Peter Moody, Richard Portugal, Monte Posner and Martin Wengrow. In admiration of more than 60 years' devotion to the Arsenal.

And to Samson and Abigail.

Arsène & Arsenal

The Quest to Rediscover Past Glories

Alex Fynn & Kevin Whitcher

VSP

Published by Vision Sports Publishing in 2014

Vision Sports Publishing
19-23 High Street
Kingston upon Thames
Surrey
KT1 1LL

www.visionsp.co.uk

ISBN: 978-1-9095-3425-4

Editors: Jim Drewett and Paul Baillie-Lane
Authors: Alex Fynn and Kevin Whitcher
Design: Neal Cobourne
All pictures: Getty Images

A CIP record for this book is available from the British Library

Printed and bound by CPI Group (UK) Ltd, Croydon, CR0 4YY

CONTENTS

Authors

Alex Fynn & Kevin Whitcher

Alex Fynn is a football consultant who has advised several clubs, including Arsenal, on media and marketing. *The Sunday Times* called him "the spiritual godfather of the Premier League." Kevin Whitcher is the editor of the highly influential Arsenal fanzine, *The Gooner,* and the author of *Gunning for the Double: The Story of Arsenal's 1997/98 Season.* The pair have previously collaborated on *The Glorious Game: Arsène Wenger, Arsenal and the Quest for Success* and *Arsènal: The Making of a Modern Superclub.*

Also by the authors:

By Alex Fynn & Kevin Whitcher
The Glorious Game
Arsènal

By Alex Fynn
The Secret Life of Football (with Lynton Guest)
Heroes and Villains (with Lynton Guest)
Out of Time (with Lynton Guest)
For Love or Money (with Lynton Guest)
Dream On (with H. Davidson)

Cantona on Cantona (with Eric Cantona)
The Great Divide (with Olivia Blair)

By Kevin Whitcher
Gunning for the Double: The Story of Arsenal's 1997/98 Season

Acknowledgements

This book could not have been written without the help of many people. To those who are quoted throughout the book, fulsome thanks are due for their time, consideration and insights. In addition, several people generously shared their specialised knowledge, notably Davan Feng on social media, Jeorge Bird on the youth scene and Lois Langton on the role of the Arsenal supporters' organisations.

Some of the information for the narrative of the season has been based on the *Online Gooner* blog of Kevin Whitcher and, of course, a number of other sites were very helpful in presenting different perspectives, chief among them were *Le Grove, Arseblog, ANR* and *Arsenal.com*.

Only when you venture abroad does the realisation come to you how well we are served by our much-maligned English media – press, radio and television. Thank you all for the informative and relevant reports. Nevertheless, the list of sources would not be complete without *L'Equipe, France Football* and the financial expertise of the Arsenal Supporters' Trust, the *Swiss Ramble* and still the most important analysis on the football business, the Deloitte Annual Review of Football Finance.

Sections of the book were read by Mel Goldberg and Lois Langton. Darren Epstein, Gareth Kegg, Peter Moody, Greville Waterman and Martin Wengrow drew the short straw and read the whole lot. All made suggestions which were invariably helpful, for which many thanks.

Jim Drewett and Toby Trotman at Vision Sports Publishing were just terrific, their encouragement and instruction invaluable. And to say that Paul Baillie-Lane was an excellent editor is to underplay his invaluable contribution to the text.

Rhoda Fynn and Lian Poleykett compensated for Alex Fynn's technical ineptitude by typing and transcribing thousands of words. The deadline could not have been met without their willing and efficient help.

Introduction

Ages ago BW (Before Wenger), I co-wrote a book, *Heroes and Villains: The Inside Story of the 1990/91 Season at Arsenal and Tottenham Hotspur*. Apparently in one of the focus groups I undertook, mainly to get an appreciation of what the supporters felt with regard to their club and their rival, I suggested that Arsenal would win the league and Tottenham the FA Cup. Though I have absolutely no recollection of such clairvoyance, I did feel, as a result of the popularity of England's 1990 World Cup exploits, that Tottenham might do something special and challenge George Graham's Arsenal, already being a top club and conceivably well positioned to repeat their 1989 league title.

The last edition of *Arsènal: The Making of a Modern Superclub* was published in 2011 and, much to my surprise, has continued to be relevant, being reprinted several times, the last as recently as June 2014. Before the 2013/14 season, I had the sentiment that this was going to be the one when Arsenal would finally break their trophy duck. So what better way to mark the event than to produce this sequel and bring the '*Arsènal*' story up to date in an entirely new book. Hence the appearance of *Arsène & Arsenal: The Quest to Rediscover Past Glories*, aka *Arsènal II*.

The missing seasons since the last edition of *Arsènal*, 2011/12 and 2012/13, are covered at the beginning of this book and set the scene for a detailed examination of the 2013/14 campaign.

With several chronological narrative chapters, interspersed with a number of key player profiles, with the aim of providing a coherent thread, the story veers off into dissecting a number of pertinent topics – namely transfers, marketing and finance, youth policies, injuries and the supporters' organisations – before concluding with the FA Cup triumph and an appraisal of the manager and his playing strategy.

A word regarding how the book was written: over the last couple of years, the time spent with the key protagonists, especially messrs Wenger and Dein, has been limited, which makes their many earlier one-to-one sessions all the more valuable. Their *verbatim* conversations and many other direct quotes, including those of Liam Brady and Alan Smith, are taken from tapes or notes made at the time. These are usually described as conversations with a friend, an acquaintance or colleague, which are my *noms de plume*.

Alex Fynn, June 2014

Chapter 1

Déjà Vu All Over Again[1]

"When we decided to build the stadium, I wanted to anticipate the possibility of financial restrictions, so I concentrated on youth," Arsène Wenger asserted in 2008. "I also felt the best way to create an identity with the way we play football, to get players integrated into our culture, with our beliefs, our values, was to get them as young as possible and to develop them together. I felt it would be an interesting experiment to see players grow together with these qualities, and with a love for the club." However, three years later Wenger was forced to attempt to reconcile these noble sentiments with the financial realities of the Premier League.

"Imagine the worst situation – we lose Fabregas and Nasri – you cannot convince people you are ambitious after that. If you

---

[1] In 1961, when it appeared that Babe Ruth's record of 60 home runs in a baseball season (1927), would never be overtaken, in a serendipitous coincidence, not one but two New York Yankees, Mickey Mantle and Roger Maris, went head to head in their efforts at setting a new landmark. (Maris established a new record of 61 and Mantle eventually ended with 54.) As one phenomenal home run followed another, their legendary teammate and master of tautology, the catcher Yogi Berra, reportedly said in wonderment, "It's a case of *déjà vu* all over again."

give that message out, you cannot pretend you are a big club, because a big club first of all holds onto its big players and gives a message to all the other big clubs that they just cannot come in and take [players] away from you. We worked very hard with these players [Fabregas and Nasri] for years to develop them, and now it is time for us to keep them together."

This was the forthright and atypical proclamation from Wenger in July 2011, perhaps intimating that he was not in tune with the directors' view that the two players represented an important and much-needed source of revenue, prime assets that should perhaps be cashed in if optimum value could be attained.

But Wenger probably knew that he was fighting a losing battle, that the departures of Fabregas and Nasri were inevitable, and that his defiant statement would come back to haunt him. And so it came to pass. Within a matter of weeks, the sale of his captain, Cesc Fabregas, to Barcelona was agreed, and then a few days later Samir Nasri joined Manchester City, where he would link up with Gael Clichy, who had joined the same club only weeks earlier. Sure, Arsenal received £55 million for the pair and £7 million for their first-choice left-back, but accusations that they were now a selling club, a feeder club for their rivals, seemed justified. In the modern era, no other leading club at home or abroad has been so reliant on player sales and property development in order to make profits. In fact, following the move to the Emirates, the income from outgoing transfers had been the main contribution to perennial profits. Chairman Peter Hill-Wood's announcement in 2012 that he was presiding over "another healthy set of full year figures" camouflaged the reality that, if the revenue from the sales of Fabregas, Nasri and Clichy had been excluded, the club would have made a substantial year end loss of more than £28 million. And with the board firmly sticking to a policy of self-sufficiency – only spending the earned revenue – unless costs, especially the wage bill, were reduced or income substantially increased, the annual policy of selling a star player or two remained the easiest option to keep the bottom line in the black. In fact, Arsenal last reported a loss over a decade ago in 2002, which is a rare feat in the dog-eat-dog world of professional football. However, they are not alone in this achievement. Barcelona and Real Madrid usually find themselves in the plus column, except when they splurge on 'galactico' style signings; Bayern Munich have been continuously profitable for even longer than Arsenal; and Manchester United usually are, and would always be, profitable were it not for the interest charges incurred as a consequence of their ownership by the Glazer family.

Throughout his trophy winning years, Nicolas Anelka aside, Arsène Wenger tended to offload his stars once he determined that he had extracted their best years from them. Barcelona paid sizeable sums for Marc Overmars and Emmanuel Petit, and later Thierry Henry, but none of them performed as well in Spain as they had in north London. The same could be said of Patrick Vieira at Juventus and Internazionale. But now the talent drain was different. Key assets were departing before they had fulfilled their potential, albeit bequeathing a huge profit; a precedent set when Manchester City took Emmanuel Adebayor (age 25) in 2009 and Gael Clichy (also age 25) in 2011.

Fabregas and Nasri were only 24 when they were sold by Arsenal. Despite having progressed season by season, they were nowhere near their peak. Meanwhile, Wenger had put his faith in the mistaken belief that the culture and status of Arsenal would transcend the enticing riches and probable trophies that more affluent and ambitious adversaries could promise, at least in the short term, which gave rise to the question: Was there anything that the manager could have tried in order to keep hold of the two of them? After working with men who shared his idealism, such as Thierry Henry, Dennis Bergkamp and Robert Pires, Wenger felt let down when their successors did not follow suit. With hindsight though, he probably realised that Nasri had been made an offer he could not refuse, while Fabregas was returning home. For both players there was more chance of winning championships and the certainty of earning more money with their new clubs. Wenger might have felt reconciled to the inevitable departures if he had mirrored the attitude of the late renowned boxer promoter and manager, Micky Duff, who advised: "If you want loyalty, buy a dog."

As Uli Hoeness,[2] one of the key members of the illustrious Bayern Munich management team, could have told him: "We don't have too many people from outside [our country] because they don't usually intend to stay here for the rest of their lives and we don't get the same commitment." However, in the last few years, as Bayern raised their sights from Germany to European hegemony, they adopted a more flexible, cosmopolitan attitude. So, Dutch international Arjen Robben and French international Franck Ribery became two of several foreign adornments to the prerequisite national nucleus. Five years after moving to a new stadium with the expressed intent of being able to compete financially with all-comers, Arsenal were weakening their stock in trade and thus falling short where it mattered most – on the pitch.

By prioritising making a profit over keeping the team together and winning trophies, the Arsenal board undoubtedly made

---

[2] Hoeness was forced to resign as president in May 2014 after being jailed for tax evasion, although he plans to return after serving his sentence.

the manager's task harder following the move to the Emirates, but with the examples of the futile extravagant spending of Leeds and Portsmouth, and the relegation suffered by clubs such as Sunderland, Derby, Leicester and Coventry, a contributory cause of which was the laudable, albeit costly, move to a new ground, the policy of self-sufficiency, if not substantial profits, could arguably be justified. The directors could point to the fact that Arsenal had exceeded expectations with the team remaining at the same high level of performance that they had been at when they moved from their old Highbury stadium.

The 2011/12 season marked Arsenal's 125th anniversary and preparations were well in hand to commemorate the event, culminating in the unveiling of three bronze statues of Herbert Chapman, Tony Adams and Thierry Henry on the podium outside the Emirates Stadium the day before the home game with Everton on 10 December, the closest league fixture to the first game played by Dial Square, Arsenal's original incarnation back in 1886.

Before all that fanfare, the celebrations commenced using the theme 'Forward', borrowed from Bernard Joy's seminal book, *Forward Arsenal*, which traced the history of the club from its formation to its seventh league title in 1953. Unfortunately, in 2011 the theme was an ambivalent choice, a hostage to fortune. Some fans were so perturbed at the summer sales of Fabregas, Nasri and Clichy that a nascent supporters' group calling themselves 'Where Has Our Arsenal Gone?' (who subsequently became known as the 'Black Scarf Movement') went to the expense of hiring a billboard facing the directors' entrance to the stadium, with a huge question mark added to the club's theme – 'Forward?' – in the hope of pricking the board's conscience and provoking a debate about the club's objectives for the season.

Less than a week after the departure of Nasri in August 2011, Arsenal travelled to Old Trafford for their third Premier League fixture of the new season. Having taken a solitary point from their opening two matches, it was hardly the ideal moment to come face to face with one of the most difficult tasks in their schedule. However, no one bar the most chauvinistic United fan could have envisaged the dramatic turn of events. The afternoon was to prove a watershed for Wenger's strategy to build a team based on his young *protégées*. Arsenal suffered the ignominy of an 8-2 drubbing, and moreover, it was inflicted by a side whose average age was six months younger than theirs. No longer could Arsène Wenger use the mitigating excuse of a youthful team in transition.

Notwithstanding notable absentees such as Bacary Sagna, Thomas Vermaelen and Kieran Gibbs, whom barring injury or suspension would have been in contention for a starting spot, the extent of the rout indicated an alarming lack of depth in the squad. According to the United manager, Sir Alex Ferguson, as he later reflected in his autobiography in a somewhat patronising manner: "It actually reached the point where I felt – please no more goals. It was a humiliation for Arsène. The climate at Arsenal was hardly serene to begin with. But we played some fantastic football that day. With the missed chances on either side, it might have been 12-4 or 12-5." It was Arsenal's worst defeat since 1896, dropped them to seventeenth place in the table and prompted a radical shake-up of Wenger's transfer policy.

There were three more days before the summer transfer window slammed shut, and having added only two reinforcements of any significance – Ivory Coast international winger Gervinho (24) from Lille and midfielder Alex Oxlade-Chamberlain (17) from Southampton – the manager undoubtedly had cash in hand. Impervious to the widespread views from bloggers, tweeters and callers to radio phone-ins that the Old Trafford debacle was irrefutable proof that he had passed his sell-by date, the man himself realised that he must radically alter his strategy. The idea that his young charges could mature and grow older and wiser together under his tutelage was brusquely put to one side as the pragmatist finally held sway over the philosopher. A brief bout of soul-searching convinced him that desperate times – the transfer window was about to close and the few available bargains and even good players at fair prices had long since been snapped up – called for the desperate expediency of prioritising experience over value for money or long-term potential.

Unusually, funds were splashed on four men in their mid and late twenties, in addition to securing an even older one on loan. Over a period of two days, ending on 31st August 2011, five deals were concluded. Midfielder Mikel Arteta (29) arrived from Everton and German international centre-back Per Mertesacker (26) from Werder Bremen, while Israeli international Yossi Benayoun (31) came on loan from Chelsea. Less familiar names were Brazilian left-back Andre Santos (28) from Fenerbahce, along with Monaco striker and South Korean captain Park Chu-Young (26). An eclectic *potpourri* of Premier League know-how and imported internationals, but the one thing they all had in common was that they were the wrong side of 25, in contrast to the manager's hitherto preference in his purchasing policy for several summers past. (The eleventh-hour nature of the signings undoubtedly adversely affected Arsenal's ability to negotiate their contracts and was thus a probable contributory factor in the 15 per cent rise in the wage bill to over £140 million from the 2010 figure.)

"When I think about what happened," reflected Martin Wengrow, a fan and shareholder of more than 50 years, "it really makes my blood boil. It was a neglected opportunity to use the transfer window properly, putting themselves [Arsenal] in a position where they felt they had to panic buy. And the chance to integrate [the new arrivals] in pre-season had been missed."

From the nadir of earning just a single point out of a possible nine from the fixtures against Newcastle, Liverpool and Manchester United, together with the loss of their two prodigies, there were now no delusions of grandeur. Any real sense of ambition had to be tempered by the reality that it would take the incomers, however experienced, time to settle with colleagues whose morale had suffered a battering. And assimilation was hardly helped by reports of a divisive cultural and linguistic divide between the 'Brits', the 'Frenchies' (as they were referred to by their own media) and the other foreign players. However, the benefit of hands-on experience was soon demonstrated as Arteta and Mertesacker reputedly took the initiative to reorganise the tables at the training ground restaurant to break down barriers and facilitate integration and team spirit. Despite only having been at the club for a short time, these two mature players demonstrated the benefit of Wenger's amended transfer policy, which henceforth would endeavour to incorporate more experienced leaders when appropriate.

On the field, a new sense of togetherness was soon increasingly evident and gradually helped to instil some consistency, although the dearth of attacking options was starkly revealed with the return in December of Thierry Henry for a short loan spell from his MLS side New York Red Bulls. Park Chu-Young, notable only for some fitful and bizarre substitute appearances in high-profile encounters against Manchester United and

AC Milan, failed to make his mark, whilst any semblance of quality had long since deserted Marouane Chamakh, a pale shadow of the striker who had led Bordeaux to the French title in 2009. Similarly, the expensive Gervinho appeared to have completely mislaid his French *Ligue 1* form and now habitually wasted gilt-edged chances. Both these Gallic imports were easy targets for the crowd's frustration, which merely aggravated their form, unlike Aaron Ramsey who appeared to be made of sterner stuff. Paradoxically, Andre Santos overlapped in the traditional Brazilian style, but this asset was counterbalanced by some abysmal defending in his primary role.

The obvious deficiencies notwithstanding, there was undeniably a growing sense of exasperation among the supporters with the apparent lack of ambition exemplified by the evident priority of a top four finish and consequential Champions League qualification, reiterated by the manager at the October AGM, rather than making a concerted bid for the title or even prioritising a trip to Wembley. The shift in attitude was clearly apparent to former manager George Graham: "He [Wenger] has raised his own bar, but he has to say to himself, 'Have I fallen a little bit?' The onus is now to qualify in the top four, whereas before that the onus was to win the Premiership."

After labouring through the group stages of the Champions League, an unfortunate draw in the round of 16 pitted Arsenal against AC Milan, and, despite a spirited 3-0 home win in the second leg, the tie was already beyond them due to a 4-0 thrashing at the San Siro. Thus, the only consolation was the windfall of around £15 million from the five Emirates games – Arsenal had overcome Udinese from *Serie A* to reach the lucrative group stage – and UEFA's exceptionally generous handout of £23 million. This comprised appearance and performance fees and a share of the English market pool (based on the rights fees paid by the UK broadcasters, ITV and Sky Television), which was divided between the four qualified Premier League clubs. The difference in amounts received was determined by the club's position in their domestic league in their qualifying season and the number of Champions League matches played in the previous campaign.

After the calamitous start to their league programme, the tide truly turned when a run of 27 points from ten matches unfolded as winter gave way to spring – including a morale-boosting 5-2 rout of Tottenham, who at the time looked set to deprive Arsenal of their habitual European spot – propelled them to a third-place finish, 19 points adrift of runners-up Manchester United. Along the way there were still some self-inflicted obstacles to be overcome, such as 2-1 defeats to both lowly QPR and Wigan, and they required a victory on the final day of the season to seal fourth place. A woeful display from debutant West Bromwich goalkeeper, Martin Fulop, who had a hand in all three of Arsenal's goals in a 3-2 defeat (which turned out to be his one and only appearance for West Brom after he was released at the end of the season), resulted in Spurs missing out on the top four by a single point, ultimately denying them a Champions League place for finishing fourth due to Chelsea winning the trophy and thereby becoming England's fourth and last representative.

With 30 league goals – and the Golden Boot as the leading Premier League marksman – Robin van Persie had been crucial in amassing the 70 points that secured third spot. The Dutch international's immense contribution could be measured by the fact that Arsenal's next highest league goalscorer was Theo Walcott, with a mere eight to his name. However, as van Persie was about to enter the final year of his contract, there was some unease over his long-term commitment to the club he had joined in 2004 as a 20 year old, particularly in the light of the departures of Fabregas and Nasri under similar circumstances.

Whether van Persie stayed or left, Arsenal could not continue their reliance on Robin and more strikers were urgently needed. Although positive progress was duly made with the procurement of Lukas Podolski from Cologne and Olivier Giroud from Montpellier, securing van Persie's services for 2012/13 and beyond remained the number one priority. Before departing for international duty with the Netherlands at the Euro 2012 tournament, van Persie met with Ivan Gazidis and Arsène Wenger to discuss his future. In hindsight, it was certainly in Arsenal's interest not to report the outcome of the discussion, and when Gazidis subsequently took part in a question and answer (Q&A) event with supporters in early June, the CEO was able to side-step the issue by saying that, although he had met with van Persie, both parties had made a personal undertaking to keep the subject confidential. "We don't want the same distractions as last summer," he added, alluding to the painfully drawn-out saga of Barcelona's pursuit of Cesc Fabregas.

Van Persie kept his counsel until after the Euros, but in early July broke his silence and confirmed the fans' worst fears. "Out of my huge respect for Mr Wenger, the players and the fans, I don't want to go into any details, but unfortunately in this meeting it has again become clear to me that we in many aspects disagree on the way Arsenal FC should move forward. I've thought long and hard about it, but I have decided not to extend my contract." An odds-on outcome when the prospect of a substantial salary rise from another club was in the offing, and one that reflected the negotiating power that the elite players such as van Persie now possessed. So, the years the club spent nurturing his talent and helping him recuperate from his many injuries counted for nothing. On the other hand, van Persie could argue that finishing fourth and qualifying for the Champions League met the board's expectations, but obviously not those of himself or the many fans who put baubles before banknotes.

During his final season at the Emirates the Dutch international was the only remaining participant from a trophy winning Arsenal team. The 2005 FA Cup was the club's most recent accomplishment and, seven years on, soon to turn 29, van Persie had decided he could not wait any longer to find out if the next season was going to be any different from most of those he had endured in north London. In retrospect, his behaviour after the final home match of 2011/12 suggested his mind may already have been made up for some time, as he had gone out of his way to have pictures of himself taken around the Emirates Stadium, probably as a memento.

Van Persie was not the first big name who was not prepared to wait around for the manager's plans to come to fruition – similar rumblings of discontent surrounded the departures of Thierry Henry and Cesc Fabregas – and his stance made a parting of the ways inevitable. How could the captain and leading man publicly disagree with the avowed direction of the club? The dye was cast. Of course, Arsenal could have forced van Persie to honour the final year of his contract, and there was a financial argument for doing so as no realistic transfer fee would come close to matching the Champions League jackpot and, without his services, or a costly world-class replacement, the failure to finish fourth in the league looked a distinct possibility. Although Arsenal's preference was to sell van Persie to a club outside the Premier League,

Juventus was the only potential buyer, and with the two Manchester clubs vying for the role of sugar daddy it was decided, to the dismay of many, to sell him to United for £25 million. Although many fans now regarded van Persie as a pariah, a more balanced view was expressed by Martin Wengrow: "From a playing and a financial point of view, his decision was a no-brainer. Almost singlehandedly, he had dragged the club into a Champions League spot when he knew he would almost certainly leave at the end of the season. He does not deserve the fans' scorn."

Commenting some months later, when Manchester United, propelled by van Persie's goals, were heading inexorably to yet another Premier League title, while Arsenal were facing a Champions League exit at the first knockout round and their perennial end of season struggle to qualify for the following tournament, Arsenal shareholder and television celebrity Piers Morgan had no compunction about blaming the club: "Do you think," he asked rhetorically, "the old Arsène Wenger, who competed so brilliantly with Manchester United, would ever have sold our best player, Robin van Persie, to Manchester United, gifting them the league, as Arsène Wenger personally did when Alex Ferguson rang him repeatedly to persuade him? And by the way, how many calls would it take Wenger to try and get Wayne Rooney out of Manchester United? The answer is a million. And then try again."

Morgan's view was corroborated by Jason Burt, the *Sunday Telegraph*'s football correspondent, who averred: "There is a huge paternalistic streak in Arsène Wenger, but sometimes he doesn't always help the club. For example, Robin van Persie leaves and it's almost as if Arsène Wenger is pushing him in the direction of Manchester United. But is that best for Arsenal? Almost like Wenger thought that is the best thing for van Persie's career." However, it does seem a more likely scenario that, having tried manfully but unsuccessfully to retain his captain, Wenger accepted the transfer as a *fait accompli*. Nevertheless, that is not to minimise the agonies he must have endured. To sell to a rival would have been deeply wounding, as he has always put the welfare of the club and the team above that of any individual, including himself.

So the new reality was that Giroud and Podolski had not been bought as supplementary strikers, but as replacements for the departing Dutch international. Would the talisman of yesterday – Bergkamp, Vieira and Henry – have countenanced a move to a Premier League rival, even if no obstacles had been placed in their path? But the team they adorned was a very different proposition to the one of 2012. They arrived at Highbury as gifted individuals and Arsène Wenger nurtured their talent, giving them the opportunity to develop into world-class players and win titles and cups for Arsenal. For them, there was no need look elsewhere, as the greenest grass always grew in Highbury.

And so the downward course continued. Reprising the two departures of the previous summer transfer window, another mainstay of the first team, midfielder Alex Song, joined Fabregas at Barcelona in August 2012, just days after the exit of van Persie. Song was another prospect who had been groomed and given protected species status, so that more mature personnel who might have hindered his development were not sought. Aged 24, he was yet one more already on his way before his peak years, his loss regretted by many fans who hitherto had been his fiercest critics, feeling that the manager had turned a blind eye to his indifferent form of past seasons. Runner-up to van Persie in the end of season poll for the player of the year, there seemed no explanation for the club selling Song other than to make a huge £14 million profit (signed from French club Bastia for £1 million and sold to Barcelona for £15 million). Although three recruits of proven quality had been acquired – the Spanish international midfielder Santi Cazorla from Malaga joined Giroud and Podolski, and left back Nacho Monreal arrived from Cazorla's old club in January 2013 – and the club had broken even in their transfer business (£47.2 million spent and £47.2 million received), Arsenal had lost its prized asset, leaving the squad bereft of indisputable star quality and pre-season optimism among the fans in short supply.

And such sentiments were shared in the dressing room. Recuperating from a broken leg, French international right-back Bacary Sagna told *L'Equipe*, the French daily sports newspaper: "We expected Robin van Persie to leave, but Alex Song, that was a surprise. I still don't understand," he said. "It is a big loss for the club. When you see last season's two best players leave, you ask yourself many questions. I understand that the supporters are irritated."

Nevertheless, change was in the air and the encouraging start to the 2012/13 season followed Steve Bould's promotion and reward of a more proactive role. An integral part of George Graham's famous backline and title-winning teams of 1989 and 1991, Bould had been promoted to assistant manager in May 2012 to replace the long-serving Pat Rice, who had retired at the end of the previous campaign. And with Neil Banfield becoming first-team coach, the backroom set-up underwent its most important evolution of the Wenger regime. In a retrospective move borrowed from the Graham era, Bould was given time to take the defence to one side in order to work on specific drills. The preceding campaign had seen 49 league goals conceded, the most in a season under Wenger's tenure, an inherent weakness that had been ignored for too long and needed to be eradicated forthwith. The belated steps forward still left a situation that was a far cry from the era when experienced internationals Jens Lehmann, Sol Campbell and Gilberto Silva, key personnel in key roles, together with input on the training pitch from their former colleague, Martin Keown, formed a defensive unit that helped take the team all the way to the 2006 Champions League final.

The opening five league matches of the season saw only two goals conceded in an unbeaten run, a visit to Anfield and the reigning champions Manchester City notwithstanding. Then, out of the blue, stories began to emerge of differences between Wenger and Bould. In his press conferences, the manager pointedly downplayed Bould's influence on the obvious defensive improvements, as if giving his assistant manager credit would be a personal indictment on his own organisa-tional skills, and apparently reduced his new assistant's input. This situation was seemingly confirmed when fitness coach Tony Colbert, rather than Bould, took charge of training in Wenger's absence, the day before an unexpected 2-0 reverse at home to Swansea in December.

Perhaps Wenger's mind had been made up a few weeks pre-viously. The nature of the 1-0 defeat to Norwich at the end of October had been the antithesis of the way Wenger expected his teams to play; lacking creativity and having few shots at goal, the performance went against the grain. According to the *Online Gooner*: "This was an Arsenal side without spirit, devoid of character... Norwich had, before yesterday, failed to win a single one of their seven league games... they should have been meat and drink to a team with top four pretensions. Arsenal lacked the intelligence to overcome poor opponents... worst of all, there was no heart, no appetite for the battle." Reflecting on this game, Wenger must have come to the conclusion that the price of defensive solidity was not worth paying if it led to such insipid displays. Once again, the priority became positive play and any defensive improvement would have to wait until lost ground had been recovered.

Nevertheless, former players were mystified at Wenger's apparent disinterest in working at defending. Alan Smith commented in disbelief: "They've let in a few goals and maybe he [Wenger] used that as an excuse. But how can working on the defence be counterproductive?" Another Arsenal old boy, 1980s midfielder Stewart Robson, was just as critical: "Being able to defend all round the field [is fundamental]. That's been my major criticism over the years. I used to do some analysis for *Arsenal TV*. I used to do it every Monday morning and I got fed up doing it because I had to say the same things week in week out [thereby ensuring that his assignment was of short-term duration]. I'd seen the same mistakes happen over a five-year period. After a while you'd think, surely, if things are going wrong in the defensive area – [for example] playing too high a line or the full-backs taking up the wrong positions – all these [errors] week after week kept happening. If you are the manager or the coach and you keep seeing it, you'd think you would try and rectify it, but it never happens." Robson summed up his reservations with the damning judgement: "I don't think Arsenal have a defensive game plan. They can be caught out of shape. They can be unbalanced. They don't have players who are good decision-makers. When a team starts to play through them and counter-attack with some intelligence, that's when Arsenal struggle."

Certainly, the team became inconsistent and dropped unexpected points after their initial good form. A late October Capital One League Cup tie away at Reading epitomised both Arsenal's unpredictability and vulnerability. At the interval, they were trailing 4-0. After the end of the second half, the scores were level, and extra time saw an astonishing four further goals, with Arsenal eventually running out 7-5 winners. Cock-eyed entertainment, but the concession of four goals in 45 minutes was a bad omen. Where were the Adams and Bould of not so long ago?

Since his arrival at Highbury in 1996, Arsène Wenger had never suffered defeat to a lower division side in the domestic cup competitions. The 2012/13 season saw the unthinkable happen, not once but twice. After scraping through at Reading, his team were drawn away at League Two side Bradford City and, despite starting with ten internationals, could only muster a 1-1 draw after extra time and were eliminated in a penalty shoot-out. Bradford's starting 11 had been put together at a cost of just £7,500 (ten being free transfers), in comparison to the visitors at over £65 million.

The indignity was compounded when, within the space of four days in February, Arsenal suffered home defeats in the FA Cup and Champions League, the two remaining competitions in which they had a theoretical chance of success. In the FA Cup fifth round, Championship side Blackburn took advantage of a weakened line-up in which key players were rested, and in an ironic turn of events the visitors' winning goal came after three habitual starters – Walcott, Cazorla and Wilshere – had been introduced in a forlorn attempt to avoid the nuisance of a replay.

The blow to morale was hardly ideal preparation for the first leg of a Champions League last 16 tie against Bayern Munich.

That February evening cruelly highlighted the chasm between Arsenal and the top teams at home and abroad. Victories over Manchester United, Chelsea and Manchester City were now few and far between, notable only for their rarity. Furthermore, their second successive demise in the first knockout round of the Champions League came via the German champions who administered a football lesson at the Emirates, with a 3-1 scoreline which flattered the hosts.

After the Bayern Munich defeat, *Daily Telegraph* football correspondent Henry Winter told BBC Radio 5 Live listeners: "Arsenal just look like they hadn't been coached. And that [criticism] has to come down to Wenger [and] who he employs. Is Steve Bould given the licence he wants to actually go and coach the defence [as he learnt] under George Graham when they had that fantastic back four? I just thought there was an alarming naivety, a lack of organisation and the key thing for me with this Arsenal team is the lack of leaders. Jack Wilshere was one of the youngest players out there and he was the only one who was [taking] the fight to Bayern Munich in the second half."

The manner of the Bayern beating unleashed a torrent of recriminations from both the fans and the media, the principal targets being the directors and their most expensive employee, Arsène Wenger, whose wages policy, centred on long-term contracts for young players, was highlighted with its dire ramifications on team selection and performance. As Henry Winter commented: "Arsenal actually have a big wage bill [in 2012 it was £143 million, only £20 million less than Manchester United, having grown by 38 per cent over the previous three years], but the problem is that it is totally unbalanced. There are some very average players on above average money – the Squillaci factor [the former French international defender, signed in the summer of 2010, being one of several whose displays did not reflect their multi-million pound purchase, in his case £4 million, or their exorbitant salaries]. Wages should be performance related. If you are doing well and you are delivering goals and assists and all the statistical things [on which] they now try and judge footballers, then that should take you above the 100 grand a week, but there are too many very average players in this club taking in crazily large sums." Many of these players were only too happy to accept their second-class status (and first-class wages) and sit on the bench, thereby making it difficult to move them out to make room for better replacements until their contracts had expired.

And as Stewart Robson noted, it was not just the quantity but the quality that was lacking: "There are a lot of other buys [in addition to Gervinho] that have to be questioned. Sebastien Squillaci, Nicklas Bendtner, Denilson, Andre Santos. These are players now playing [on loan] all around the world on massive money which Arsenal are paying a lot of because they were bad signings. The network of scouts [Wenger] once had don't seem to be working these days."

George Graham made the same point when he asked: "Who is bringing the players to the club? The quality is the problem. I think over the last few seasons the standard has slipped only because the players coming into the club are just inferior to the players who were there years ago." Although superstars such as Bergkamp, Henry and Pires come along once in a lifetime and to compare them to the current generation is unrealistic and unfair, the likes of Lauren, Toure, Ljungberg and Gilberto Silva, who were all essential elements of successful Arsenal sides, had certainly not been adequately replaced.

Defeat at White Hart Lane less than a fortnight after the Bayern encounter left the prospect of a return to the Champions League the following season looking like a lost cause, with Tottenham in third, Chelsea in fourth and Arsenal five points adrift of the last qualification spot. After controlling the game, Arsenal succumbed to two embarrassing defensive errors and lost 2-1. "It's a shame about the inability to defend as 11 men," lamented the *Online Gooner*, "because Arsenal actually played fairly well, [but] as long as they don't get the basics right, they are going to struggle."

Wenger realised that more time had to be given to defensive preparation. As Per Mertesacker recalled after the post-match debrief: "There was a lot of room for improvement and we saw a lot of [wrong] things on television. Sometimes we didn't choose the right direction and we just lacked a bit of defensive work as a unit. You have a different view on the pitch. Sometimes you can't believe what you did as a defensive unit. Everyone felt we needed to improve and speak [communicate with each other]." Not least Wenger and Bould, who, seated side by side on the bench, gave the appearance of two strangers forced to share two seats on a bus in rush hour.

The postponement of a Premier League fixture against Everton in early March 2013 due to the Merseysiders' FA Cup involvement gave some much needed time for recuperation and reflection, and when Arsenal returned to the fray a more pragmatic approach appeared to be the order of the day, reprising the discipline of autumn when the side looked less exposed and were less inclined to speculative assaults. Mertesacker and Laurent Koscielny resumed their central defensive partnership at the expense of Thomas Vermaelen. Despite Mertesacker's lack of pace, his calm reading of the game and organisational skills dovetailed nicely with Koscielny's speed and wholeheartedness. As Tony Adams succinctly remarked: "You need to play with your mate on a regular basis to gain confidence and I think that really worked for Arsenal."

The return leg of the Champions League tie in Munich saw a spirited display culminating in an unexpected 2-0 victory. That the second goal was scored in the final minutes meant that there was little serious threat that the deficit could be overcome (ensuring an exit at the round of 16 for the third year in succession), but it was nevertheless an astonishing result – Bayern's first home defeat for over a year – which must have been a huge boost to morale.

Now, with no distractions to their league programme and ten games remaining, the side buckled down and performed in a way that prioritised positive results rather than plaudits. Reminiscent at times of the best of the George Graham days, the defensive improvement suggested Steve Bould had resumed his chores. Alan Smith, his former teammate, welcomed Bould's involvement but felt he had a lot more to offer: "I think he has had a big influence because he does some coaching, but not as much as an assistant with his background might do at another club. Arsène Wenger, over all the years he has been there, has worked in a certain fashion and he doesn't tend to concentrate on going through defensive drills. But if you bring in someone like Steve Bould, what's the point if you don't use his expertise? Not just through sessions he might do with them, but his words of advice where he pulls people to one side."

Whatever the truth of the matter, the team went on an undefeated run of ten matches, surrendering only four points in home draws with Everton and Manchester United. There were some close shaves, some narrow wins and plenty of determined defending, and the denouement arrived away at Newcastle. Needing three points to be sure of securing fourth place and the much sought-after Champions League qualification, they were duly achieved courtesy of a solitary goal from Laurent Koscielny and celebrated with a self-satisfied vigour that suggested they had turned the tables on the many critics who had written them off just weeks ago. A campaign which had yielded three more points than the previous season, putting Arsenal one place lower and only 16 points behind the runaway champions, Manchester United, could, through rose-coloured spectacles, be viewed positively. Once more, Tottenham finished a point behind, understandably crestfallen after attaining 72 points, yet still only receiving the booby prize of a Europa League place. A case of *déjà vu* all over again.

The prospect of yet another Champions League campaign for the fifteenth successive year and the guaranteed £40 million injection to the bottom line, coupled with new sponsorship and merchandising agreements from Emirates and Puma (a new kit supplier who would replace Nike at the start of the 2014/15 season), encouraged an optimistic approach. CEO, Ivan Gazidis, declaimed: "We are an extraordinarily ambitious club [and] we should be able to compete at a level like a club such as Bayern Munich." With the new three-year Premier League television deals from Sky and BT commencing in 2013/14 (a 70 per cent rise on the previous sum, which amounted to a staggering total with the inclusion of the overseas deals of around £5.7 billion), the Premier League's status as the pre-eminent European league was comfortably maintained. Arsenal, as one of the leading clubs, could envisage, on top of the previous season's £57.1 million, an additional minimum of £25 million from just the domestic deals, with maybe another £10 million when the overseas revenue was fully realised, which should take their Premier League broadcast income for 2014 above the £90 million mark.

Although the German *Bundesliga* had secured its own improved broadcast deal, it still languished behind its English counterpart, obtaining just over a quarter of the amount of the Premier League at £538 million per annum. Bayern had long since recognised their comparative broadcast shortfall against their main European rivals and sought to alleviate the handicap by developing their commercial activities. By so doing they created an exceptionally strong business. Focusing on their Bavarian roots with the help of a seemingly endless list of club stalwarts and German internationals – Franz Beckenbauer, Karl-Heinz Rummenigge, Uli Hoeness, Sepp Maier and Gerd Muller being only the most distinguished – they built a strong parochial base. These living legends actually control the day-to-day business of the club and their presence is a constant reminder of the legacy of greatness they have bestowed. Thus winning is not everything, it is the only thing, and has been the *raison d'être* of the club for decades.

Back in 2000 Hoeness summed up quite simply by saying, "We have to abolish losing." And Rummenigge added, "We ask whether a new player is really confident. Is he willing to believe that the team must be perfect?" For their part, Arsenal should take a leaf out of Bayern's book and not repeat the lost opportunity of capitalising on the leadership qualities of the double-winning captains Frank McLintock and Tony Adams. While time may have been called on the former, is the latter such a loose cannon that a position on the coaching staff could not be conjured for both the club's and former stalwart's mutual benefit? Arsenal have found it easier to erect a statue for Adams than give him a job. Further, when the time is right for Wenger to put aside his managerial duties, he could surely fulfil the Beckenbauer/Rummenigge role; a wise and experienced elder statesman who would not be a threat to his successors because of his undying commitment to the club. But will he be given the opportunity?

The aim constantly to refresh and rejuvenate the playing squad through a judicious amalgam of Germanic youth, *Bundesliga* experience and bought-in talent has taught Bayern how they can build upwards from a base of the home grown contingent. Can Arsène Wenger's attempt to build a strong core of British players – Wilshere, Walcott, Oxlade-Chamberlain, Gibbs, Jenkinson and Ramsey – ever emulate the indigenous nucleus of Manuel Neuer, Philipp Lahm, Jerome Boateng, Bastian Schweinsteiger, Thomas Muller, Tony Kroos and Mario Gomez to name just seven of the German champions? Moreover, as anyone at Bayern will tell you, a successful team (a consummate quintuple in 2013 of German league and cup, Champions League, UEFA Super Cup and FIFA World Club Championship) is the prerequisite to a successful business; Bayern's commercial turnover, at over £200 million, was more than three times that of Arsenal (the German club's total revenue of £370 million was £90 million more than their London rivals) and the club has been in profit for 20 successive seasons. No need to sell their best players or become residential property developers. By any criterion, in comparing themselves to Bayern, Arsenal have set themselves a laudable objective, but hopefully they realise that they have a long road to travel and an unchallengeable first step would be to immediately strengthen the playing resources. Everything starts from there. And they unquestionably have the means to do so.

At the end of the 2012/13 season Arsenal's cash reserves were an enviable £153 million. The combined total of those of the other 19 Premier League clubs was just shy of £200 million. Arsenal had more cash than any other European club, most of whom tended to keep less in hand and preferred to invest much of the available funds in strengthening their playing squads. Conversely of all the Premier League clubs, only Manchester United, as a result of the borrowing that financed the Glazer family takeover, carry more debt than Arsenal, though Arsenal's is as a result of loans required to fund the £390 million Emirates Stadium. Although the debt has been gradually reduced – increases in operating profits make it eminently manageable – provision has had to be made for interest payments and a debt servicing reserve. Even when these penurious obligations are set aside, there still remained an enormous amount – in excess of £50 million – for player acquisition and attendant wages. Indeed, a similar sum had been at the manager's disposal for some time, but he had declined to use it. With the CEO's frank talk of ambition and desire to challenge all and sundry, it was surely time to ring some changes.

Chapter 2

To Buy or Not to Buy, That is the Question

"David," said a friend of the former Arsenal vice-chairman, "when you and Arsène worked together, Arsenal didn't have the problem with transfers that they do now. Why do you think that is?"

"'Pass," replied Dein.

"Come on," persisted his friend. "If you'd been around, you would surely have said to Arsène, 'don't worry about [Mark] Schwarzer's price at his age or the extra for [Xabi] Alonso, I'll deal with the board,' wouldn't you?"

"Yes, I'd like to think so," said Dein.

"You and Arsène are really good friends, you see each other regularly. So why hasn't Arsène asked you if you want to come back?"

"The subject has never come up," said Dein.

Well, it certainly should have done. Time is a panacea – Dein was fired in 2007 – and the estrangement from the board led by Chairman Peter Hill-Wood and the late Danny Fiszman, Dein's former friend and confidante but latterly implacable opponent, could have been expected to evaporate with their departures in 2013 and 2011 respectively. What heinous crimes could David Dein have committed against the club that he loved so dearly – his wife Barbara called it "his mistress" – so as to prevent his return? Clearly, he should not have broken ranks with his fellow directors in order to woo Stan Kroenke when the American businessman was *persona non grata*. However, subsequent events have shown that he was merely being prescient, with his former colleagues paving the way after Dein's dismissal for the US sports entrepreneur to become Arsenal's majority shareholder in 2011. Where Dein led, others followed, just as they had with the appointment of Arsène Wenger, who was initially rejected by Peter Hill-Wood in 1995 in favour of Bruce Rioch until common sense prevailed the following year. Of course, there was the possibility that Dein's eldest son, Darren, whose representation of a number of key players, such as Thierry Henry, Cesc Fabregas and Robin van Persie, created a conflict of interest for the vice-chairman. But if so, the board as a whole were culpable of turning a blind eye to Dein junior's work and allowing the arrangement to continue.

Head cook and bottle washer in comparison to his fellow managers at other top clubs, Arsène Wenger has been given too much power. As the Arsenal Supporters' Trust observed as far back as December 2012: "One man cannot direct all transfer targets, wages, coaching methods and manage the team at games. It is too much for one man." And George Graham concurred: "The game has got bigger. His [Wenger's] job has got bigger, so he cannot do everything. Whether he can do the job he did when he first came to Arsenal, I don't know."

Wenger undeniably missed David Dein's support and input. As co-partners in a common cause, they had together secured players such as Thierry Henry, Robert Pires and Sol Campbell, all of whom would become mainstays of the manager's peerless sides. It is unreasonable to expect a man, however obsessed he is with the game, to have the time and knowledge to be the expert negotiator that Dein was in the cut and thrust world of player recruitment. Reluctant to delegate, Wenger's priority has always been coaching and match preparation. He needs help with transfers. With the ever-increasing number of Premier League signings arriving from overseas, specialist knowledge and contacts in a worldwide business is indispensible to running a successful buying and selling operation. Without this know-how, it is impossible to ascertain the true value of a star performer, and it is therefore understandable why some Premier League clubs, most notably Manchester City, Tottenham and Chelsea, have gone down the continental route and appointed directors of football.

Arsenal justified the atypical eleventh-hour summer splurge in 2011 (bringing Mertesacker, Arteta, Santos, Park and Benayoun to the club over the course of two days) as a necessary one-off circumstance, but one that could so easily have been avoided with a modicum of sensible pre-planning and direct action. Following the FA Cup and Champions League exits to Blackburn and Bayern Munich respectively in February 2013, the need for a top-class defensive midfielder, striker and goalkeeper were underlined. Etienne Capoue of Toulouse, Stevan Jovetic of Fiorentina and Liverpool's Pepe Reina were identified as feasible summer targets. Needless to say, none of them materialised.

Six months later, in July 2013, there could be no trumped up excuse of insufficient funds. Ivan Gazidis had told supporters' groups a month earlier that money was available to pay the market rate for, to use Wenger's words, "top, top players", and thus any failure to bring in one, or indeed two or three, could be laid squarely at the manager's door. Unfortunately, the possession of an open chequebook has not diminished the pride that Wenger takes in lining the club's pockets, which is why he feels he warrants his astronomical annual salary of £8 million: "I am on a very good contract," he said in January 2009. "I am one of the few managers who makes money for my club every year. That is most important. I tell you something, if I would not make money for the club, I would not be on a very good contract." And Wenger's self-imposed stringent financial sacrificing that determines his transfer policy suits the directors down to the ground. "He treats our money as if it was his own," observed a delighted Peter Hill-Wood in 2011, and by all accounts Wenger has continued to do so.

With no David Dein around "to do my dirty work for me," as Wenger once described his friend's role in dealing with agents and the minutiae of contract negotiation, there was no one to nudge the manager into action. His habitual prevarication invariably meant that targets were missed and the dithering was compounded by a reluctance to countenance any realistic spending at the highest level. Praised in the past for his meticulous attention to detail, the transfer market in 2013 no longer afforded the time and space for such a measured approach. Now anyone who failed to appreciate its endemic cut and thrust nature, who lingered over closing a deal, would lose out.

"We are now going to have to pay market rates for top players," said Ivan Gazidis in June 2013. "If we are going to be a world-class football team, our wage structure will have to evolve. Arsène is on board with that. Arsène is not afraid to pay world-class players world-class salaries." Fine words in theory, but you have to acquire the players first, and to do that Wenger would have to – as the increasingly heard instruction by the fans at the Emirates went –"Spend some f***ing money." But the call to arms was ignored until 2nd September 2013, the last day of the transfer window. Moreover, until that one moment, there was never a question of approving any over-spending in order to ensure that a prime target could be ensnared. On the contrary, unrealistic offers continued to be made. There had been no discernible change in policy since 2011 when the club was brusquely rebuffed by Bolton in their attempts to sign central defender Gary Cahill. Entering the final year of his contract, Cahill was available for around £12 million. The Arsenal bid for him was low enough – less than half the asking price – for Bolton to take exception, and subsequent media reports represented Arsenal as parsimonious and out of touch with the marketplace. The Bolton manager at the time, Owen Coyle, confirmed that: "There was a conversation between Phil Gartside [Bolton chairman] and a representative of Arsenal. I'm only passing this on as a third party, but the word derisory doesn't even cover it. It's not just short, it is a million miles off, nowhere near the starting point even. When I make an offer for a player, I like to think in the right ballpark, but this wasn't even close." Cahill was subsequently sold the following January to Chelsea for a fee of £7 million, became a mainstay of their defence, won a Champions League winner's medal and graduated to a regular starting position in the England national side.

"The quality is the problem," observed George Graham in March 2013. "The quality that is coming in now is not of the quality when he [Wenger] first came." Unwilling to stump up the entry fee, while his rivals both at home and abroad have, on the contrary, acquired 'the top, top players' – in the case of Chelsea and Manchester City in job lots – Arsenal appeared to have been left by the wayside.

However, during pre-season 2013/14 there was sufficient talk to stir the interest of even the most pessimistic of the Arsenal faithful that discussions with Real Madrid regarding forwards Angel di Maria and Gonzalo Higuain, which eventually focussed on the latter, might actually lead somewhere positive. With Real Madrid coach Carlo Ancelotti's preference for Karim Benzema as the main strike partner for Cristiano Ronaldo, and with the emerging talents of Alvaro Morata and Jese Rodriguez as back-up, Higuain was available – at a price. The Argentine international would bring with him a scoring record of 107 *La Liga* goals in 190 appearances and a similar strike rate for his national side. Naturally though, there was the ritual haggling over the fee. Arsenal cynics might suggest that one of the reasons for the protracted nature of the discussions was that £100,000 in wages could be chalked off with every week that went by. They might also wonder whether there was a plan to try and subsidise the purchase by first offloading Marouane Chamakh and Gervinho (who both subsequently departed for £1 million and £8 million in early August to Crystal Palace and Roma respectively), thereby further substantially reducing the wage bill. Extreme cynics might even suggest that the reluctance to spend was further influenced by the need to ensure qualification for the group stages of the Champions League and its accompanying windfall, rather than buying early in order to increase the chances of winning the play-off tie against the Turkish champions, Fenerbahce.

The drawn-out nature of the saga invariably led to brinkmanship in testing the patience of the sellers in Madrid. So it was no surprise that the price was bumped up from £22 million, which of course Arsenal declined to pay, once Napoli's president, Aurelio De Laurentiis, arrived on the scene. Flush from having received £55 million from Paris St Germain for Edinson Cavani, he was able to splash £34 million on Higuain to replace him and still put money in the bank, leaving the Gunners well and truly gazumped. Perhaps another 'top, top player' who David Dein would not have allowed to slip through his fingers? The outcome was reminiscent of the case of the then Valencia player, Juan Mata, who thought he was Emirates bound in the summer of 2011, only for the club to prevaricate, the result of which was that he moved to Chelsea instead. Dick Law, the appropriately named lawyer who is the usual Arsenal conduit in transfer talks, spent over a week at the time in Costa Rica concentrating on the signing of forward Joel Campbell, who has yet to start a match for the club after initially being refused a work permit. (Campbell has bided his time on loan in France, Spain and Greece, at Lorient, Real Betis and Olympiakos respectively.) As pre-season began in earnest, Arsenal were left with 21-year-old Yaya Sanogo, signed on a free transfer from French second division club Auxerre, as the only recruit.

A couple of weeks earlier on the July tour to Indonesia, Vietnam and Japan, Wenger had been at pains to lower expectations of his purchasing ambitions, stressing how difficult the transfer market was in Europe where there is "a lot of money and not many players." But options nearer home never materialised either. Reports that Marouane Fellaini had been persuaded by his former Everton teammate, Mikel Arteta, to consider moving south to join him proved false, as did the rumour that Ashley Williams, the Swansea captain and central defender, had actually agreed terms with Arsenal.

Perhaps Ivan Gazidis reminded his manager of his bullish claim a couple of months earlier when he declared that Arsenal were able "to compete with any club in the world." Whatever the reason, in an astonishing move, totally out of character, Arsenal bid £40 million and £1 for Luis Suarez, believing that the extra single pound would invoke a clause in the striker's contract whereby he was able to seek a transfer from Liverpool. Unfortunately, his employers' interpretation of the clause differed, namely that they were merely under the obligation to inform their player of any offer of over £40 million which, as it was already public knowledge, effectively, in their view, rendered the clause meaningless. The Professional Footballers' Association was consulted and concurred with Liverpool's view that the clause meant that a bid over £40 million only signified "a minimum figure from which they will consider negotiation." Despite almost tripling Arsenal's previous highest transfer fee (£15 million for Andrey Arshavin in 2009), the offer was seen as opportunistic and provocative and was treated with indifference, prompting John W. Henry, Liverpool's principal owner, to tweet: "What do you think they are smoking over there at Emirates?"

With cash to splash – estimated by the erudite financial blogger the *Swiss Ramble* as a conservative £70 million – Arsenal could easily have offered £50 million for Suarez, thereby forcing Liverpool to take the bid seriously and consider whether they were being offered a more than fair price for someone who, despite his undoubted ability, might be more trouble than he was worth having already severely tested their patience and tolerance. (After having been found guilty of racist abuse, Suarez was in the middle of a further

FA indictment, another hefty fine and lengthy ban, ten games, for biting Branislav Ivanovic of Chelsea, and thus would miss the opening six games of the new campaign.) However, Wenger's innate distaste for overspending, even when he was presented with a 'put up or shut up' choice – which was probably the case with regard to the fees being required to secure either Higuain or Suarez – inevitably saw Arsenal end up with neither. Arsenal fanzine *The Gooner* succinctly summed up the ambivalence felt by the fans: "Suarez represents many things – a lot of them undesirable – but if he scores goals that bring Arsenal a trophy after so many barren seasons, he will be forgiven quickly enough." In the event, there was nothing to forgive. The Premier League goals of Luis Suarez (31 in 33) and Daniel Sturridge (21 in 29) sent Liverpool careering up the table to the runners-up spot in the 2013/14 season and rewarded Suarez with the twin accolades of both the Professional Footballers' Association and Football Writers' Association Player of the Year Award. Moreover, the fact that Suarez's exceptional strike rate did not prevent Sturridge from enjoying a similarly prolific season perhaps indicated that Giroud would have scored just as many goals as Suarez's partner as he subsequently did as a lone striker (16 in 36), and Arsenal would most likely have been crowned champions with the two of them in harness.

So Arsenal ploughed on regardless and attempted to make signings in their own way, but were severely handicapped by the fact that the manager was only prepared to pay what he believed prospective targets were worth. Naturally, this usually resulted in offers falling short of the asking price and there was no one around to make Wenger see sense. Arsenal, like many English clubs, tended to be reactive rather than proactive in their approach to acquiring players – the most important task for any club – by relying on proposals and information from agents rather than having a specific plan. The only validation that Wenger could make for this somewhat lackadaisical approach was his erroneous belief that, although new recruits might be welcome, they were not essential in order for him to challenge for honours. He was predictably upbeat when questioned about the lack of signings after a 2-2 draw with Napoli in the Emirates Cup two weeks before the season kicked off in earnest, stating: "I am confident. Why should I sit here and say to you we can absolutely not win the title with the players we have?" But in the immortal words of Mandy Rice-Davies, "He would say that, wouldn't he?"

One problem of Arsenal's own making was that it did not appear that Dick Law had the authority to complete transfer deals without the manager's approval. In theory, neither had David Dein in the past. But unlike Law, who is from the USA, Dein was steeped in European football culture and on first name terms with all the movers and shakers, presidents, sporting directors and top agents; he would have had a good idea of what any prospect might be worth and, most importantly, what Wenger might be prepared to pay. Further, the close personal relationship between the two would have encouraged Dein to be flexible and use his initiative without waiting for the green light from the manager. On one occasion, last minute negotiations resulted in Dein having to hastily make notes on the back of an envelope. On his return, after the debrief, Wenger picked up the scrap of paper, scrutinised the scribble and, with a wry grin, said to his friend, "It's only a small bit of paper, but there are some very large figures on it." It is easy to believe that working as a partnership in a spirit of harmony – "We were a duo," said Dein – that they would have avoided Arsenal's habitual transfer tribulations. Wenger's pre-eminent status (he was reported to have had a hand in the appointment of Ivan Gazidis, his own boss) would make the role of an independent sporting director untenable. However, they palpably need someone of David Dein's ilk to, in the former vice-chairman's own words, "seal the deal."

In the summer of 2013, with obvious holes to be filled at centre-back, defensive midfield and striker, and maybe goalkeeper as well, the clock was ticking down to the opening day of the season. The pre-season Asian tour and the Emirates Cup had been and gone, and the opportunity to integrate any arrivals before the first league encounter on 18th August had disappeared. Wenger's comment on the difficulty of buying players because "some clubs acted very early so the choices are reduced" seemed barely credible, given that he had the funds to use as soon as the transfer window opened.

The home defeat by Aston Villa in the first game of the 2013/14 season was a bolt from the blue, an unexpected reverse which brought home the cost of wilfully ignoring defensive deficiencies and the lack of striking options whilst millions of pounds lay idle. Three days later, and things were a lot brighter in Arsène's world following the Champions League qualifying play-off match in Istanbul; the competent manner of the 3-0 victory was just as unforeseen as the abysmal home defeat in north London. With the second leg a seeming formality and entry to the Champions League group stage ostensibly assured, there was renewed optimism amongst the fans that there was no longer any excuse not to spend on reinforcements; better the right eleventh-hour purchases than none at all. But Arsène being Arsène, Arsenal did not make it easy for themselves.

Their domestic rivals who had experienced football men in the role of sporting directors, such as Txiki Begiristain at Manchester City, Franco Baldini at Tottenham and Michael Emenalo at Chelsea, working to a strategy which incorporated specific named targets (some of whom were the result of initiatives by the sporting directors rather than the managers), had done their shopping early. This removed a number of candidates from the market who would have been on Arsenal's list and, at least on paper, their rivals appeared to be considerably stronger as a result.

No such foresight was apparent at the Emirates. The defeat to Aston Villa triggered the Pavlovian response to try and add yet another creative midfielder, in this instance French international Yohan Cabaye of Newcastle. In an uncanny echo of the Gary Cahill scenario in the summer of 2011, the £10 million bid was dismissed as "derisory' and Newcastle owner, Mike Ashley, reportedly responded to the offer with the words, "Which part of him do you want to buy?" Cabaye subsequently left in January 2014 for Paris St Germain, who willingly paid £19 million, almost twice the amount Arsenal had offered.

A week later, a reversal of the opening day scoreline in Arsenal's favour saw three points taken against Fulham at Craven Cottage, and with the comfortable return leg victory against Fenerbahce and confirmation that the Champions League pot of gold was once again guaranteed, the opening day ignominy was put into some sort of perspective. Maybe it had just been a bad dream, a false dawn and all was right in the Wenger household, particularly after a sudden stroke of fortune. A free agent after being released by AC Milan, Mathieu Flamini had been training at his old stomping ground – he had controversially departed Arsenal on a free transfer in the summer of

2008 – to recover enough fitness to put himself in the shop window and had so impressed his former boss that he was signed with alacrity on 29 August. Wenger was won over by Flamini's repentance for leaving the ship in the first place and, more relevantly, by his versatility and experience: "He can cover many positions, he knows the game we want to play, he is tactically very assured and very focussed to win. The decision was basically a no-brainer. He's 29 and the best years are in front of him, the next three years. Physically he is perfect."

Ignoring the claims that the defensive and striking positions needed his attention – maybe he was distracted by a resourceful and victorious 1-0 rearguard display at home against Tottenham on 1 September and the improved strike rate of Olivier Giroud, which banished the spectre of the opening day horror – Wenger indulged in his hobby and, though already possessing Rosicky, Cazorla, Ramsey, Wilshere and Oxlade-Chamberlain, felt compelled to add yet another creative midfielder to his collection. In mitigation, he had lost Oxlade-Chamberlain and Lukas Podolski to what turned out to be long-term injuries before August was out, but with the numbers of midfield choices at his disposal, yet another one was less of a priority than elsewhere, even taking into account that Podolski had been employed as a forward on occasions.

Real Madrid, in order to balance their books and exasperated with the manner that Tottenham were conducting the eventual world record sale of Gareth Bale for the astounding sum of £80 million – and suspicious that an aspect of the drawn-out nature of the deal might have been to prevent their north London neighbours having the same opportunity to shop in Madrid – offered Mesut Ozil to Arsenal. (Subsequent media reports suggested that Tottenham had attempted to insert a clause in the Bale deal that would have prevented Real from selling any one of four named players – Ozil, Angel di Maria, Karim Benzema and Fabio Coentrao – to any other English club before the summer of 2014). In a rush of blood, Arsenal agreed to hand over almost three times more than they had ever paid previously, namely £42.5 million, to obtain Ozil on the final day of the transfer window. Perhaps the realisation that Suarez could have been bought if they had been a little more forthcoming encouraged the board to put pressure on Wenger to buy; failure to do so would have flown in the face of Ivan Gazidis's commitment, leading in turn to undoubtedly cause an acrimonious backlash from the supporters. But however suitable Ozil turns out to be, his price was outrageously excessive, if only compared to the shopping spree of Manchester City, whom Wenger was fond of saying he could not compete with financially. In the City squad for 2013/14 there were ten players – Aguero, Fernandinho, Dzeko, Milner, Silva, Toure, Lescott, Nasri, Jovetic and Negredo – each of whom cost more than £20 million, but not one cost more than £35 million (Aguero), and Arsenal should be so lucky if Ozil matches the performances and the value for money of £25 million magician David Silva.

Only Wenger knows why the German international playmaker was not recruited when he was available at Werder Bremen. Transferred to Real Madrid in 2010 for the comparatively modest sum of around £15 million following a successful World Cup – Wenger must have watched most of his displays at first hand in his role as the main pundit for the French television broadcaster TF1 – Ozil was one of the stars of the tournament. Over the previous five years no one in the major European leagues (England, Spain, Germany, Italy and France) had made more assists. His ambidextrous versatility saw him fill roles on both flanks, as well as his favoured number 10 position, with equal ease. Whatever the reservations, there was no doubt that Arsène had finally woken up and made his first statement of genuine ambition since the club had left Highbury.

The signing sent a clear message that Arsenal were back in business, paying more than lip service about competing for trophies once again. Many fans compared Ozil's arrival to that of Dennis Bergkamp in 1995, bringing to mind that it was only when Wenger was able to play the Dutch international's calling card when he took charge of the club in 1996 that sublimity in the form of Vieira, Petit and Overmars arrived within the space of 12 months, soon to be accompanied by the trophies they helped to acquire. Significantly, Ozil's former teammates in Madrid, including Cristiano Ronaldo, lamented his departure. A Spanish newspaper reported Ronaldo as saying: "The sale of Ozil is bad news for me. He was the player who best knew my moves in front of goal. I'm angry about Ozil leaving." Closer to home, the newly reinstalled Chelsea manager, Jose Mourinho, sensed that there now might be more of a threat across town than he originally envisaged and blocked any proposed loan deal for his striker, Demba Ba.

One swallow though, however appealing, does not make a summer. The beneficial influence that Ozil without doubt had on his new teammates could not camouflage the thinness of a squad that would assuredly struggle to cope at the very top once injuries and suspensions took their inevitable toll. The lack of front-rank choices in the central defensive and striker positions was a continuing cause for concern, although fans hoped that the club could get by until the January transfer window when they would get a further opportunity to address these areas.

Five months on, as 2013 came to an end with the Gunners sitting proudly at the top of the table, the early season reservations could be viewed as unduly pessimistic. Nevertheless, the pre-eminent position was owed more to the fact that the better-equipped squads – Chelsea, Manchester City, Liverpool and certainly Tottenham – had not yet performed at their peak and worryingly appeared in better shape for the inevitable end of season dogfight. So as the January 2014 transfer window opened, Arsenal were given yet another chance to fill the gaps in their make-up – a chance that Arsène Wenger passed up.

Signing a major striker should have been a priority, in spite of the points gained during the first half of the season. Manchester City had Aguero, Dzeko and Negredo; Chelsea had Eto'o, Torres and Ba; Liverpool had Suarez and Sturridge; but Arsenal's strike force consisted of Giroud, Bendtner and Sanogo. Theoretically, the South Korean forward Park Chu-Young could have been added to the list as he did make the substitutes' bench on more than one occasion in the final months of 2013. However, he never got on the pitch and a loan deal to Watford at the same time that Arsenal were trying to get hold of a striker confirmed that his prospects were non-existent. When the January 2014 transfer window opened for business, all three forwards who were credible contenders for selection were injured and were soon joined by the unfortunate long-term casualty, Theo Walcott. Could there have been a more appropriate time or need to buy a striker? Not according to Wenger, despite having his cards marked by a senior colleague, who in a prescient comment observed weeks before the window: "Olivier Giroud won't be able to go on all alone until the end of the season. We need to buy."

Giroud had made an immense contribution. Besides scoring his fair share of goals (11 in 27 games in all competitions up to the turn of the year), the curse of missing chances in big games, which had been a feature of his play in his first season, seemed to be consigned to the past with conversions against Tottenham and Borussia Dortmund. Even when not on the scoresheet, every match saw how vital his input was: holding the ball up, laying it off adroitly, winning headers and pressurising his opponents both in attack and defence. Without Giroud for the home game against Cardiff on New Years Day 2014, Arsenal laboured until Nicklas Bendtner scored in added time, but unfortunately conspired to extend the length of the match by injuring himself in the process. With Giroud and Bendtner now both unavailable, surely the signing of another forward was just a matter of days away.

However, Wenger had his eye on Julian Draxler of Schalke, yet another attacking midfielder (albeit at least his height and languid style offered a sharp contrast to the busy approach of the vertically challenged existing midfield personnel). Unfortunately, Draxler was out of action for the foreseeable future, though propensity to injury did not prevent Wenger from signing Kim Kallstrom on loan from Spartak Moscow as his only recruit for the remainder of the season. Despite a chronic back condition, which would ultimately delay his debut until the final week in March, Kallstrom appeared in theory a reasonable stopgap for a position that seemed to attract either injury or suspension. (Maybe this last experience finally persuaded Wenger to rid himself of his predilection for luxury midfielders. No longer required by Barcelona after the conclusion of the 2013/14 *La Liga* season, as per their sale agreement Arsenal were offered first refusal on Cesc Fabregas. To the chagrin of many supporters, and Fabregas himself,

Wenger passed on the opportunity, content with earning a bonus of £5.6 million for his employers as part of the sell-on process. In June 2014, Fabregas subsequently signed for Chelsea in a deal worth around £30 million.)

So, in practice the sum total of Arsenal's transfer business for the 2013/14 season amounted to a superstar, an experienced free agent and one free signing for the future in the summer, plus an injured campaigner on loan in January. Was that all that there really was to show for the club's new-found wealth and the challenging claims by the CEO?

Ostensibly, Arsenal were unwilling to learn from past mistakes. In February 2008, they were five points clear at the top of the table when Eduardo broke his leg at Birmingham, and subsequent fixtures which hitherto could be regarded as safe bankers turned into draws due to a lack of firepower. Despite amassing 83 points that season, Arsenal were overhauled by Chelsea and the eventual champions, Manchester United. In January 2014, Lazio reportedly turned down a £2 million offer from Arsenal to take Germany's prolific international goalscorer, Miroslav Klose, on loan till the end of the season. Was the price really too high when the good fortune of the FA Cup draw had given Arsenal a fifth round home tie against Liverpool (after two home matches in the previous rounds) and an unexpected bonus that could have paid for most of an increased fee of £3 million which should have secured their man? And there were other possible candidates who were just ignored: the Swedish international striker, Ola Toivonen, had fallen out with PSV Eindhoven and was sold to Stade Rennes in *Ligue 1* for £2.1 million. Rennes had unexpectedly struggled in the first half of the season, but with Toivonen's help (six goals and one assist in nine starts) they had moved clear of the relegation places by the end of March.

The striker could have been employed as a foil or even a replacement for Giroud. He was certainly someone who Arsenal must have been aware of and who could have aided their cause.

It is one thing to have bought badly to address obvious defaults, that at least shows willing – for example, the eleventh-hour purchases of Mertesacker, Arteta and Benayoun (the relative successes of the five men drafted in at the time) after the 8-2 Manchester United fiasco in 2011 – but it is quite another to ignore salient weaknesses, not once but twice. This lack of action left the directors, and particularly the manager and the scouting staff, open to charges of indolence; a case of not finding the right players and then refusing to compromise in the belief that no improvement could be made to existing resources. From 2005 to 2014 all the top English clubs had massively outspent Arsenal on transfers. Manchester City spent £694 million, Chelsea spent £600 million, Tottenham spent £448 million, Liverpool spent £444 million, Manchester United spent £383 million. And Arsenal spent just £218 million, nearly a fifth of which was outlayed on one recruit. At the start of the January window, Arsène Wenger stated: "We are like many clubs, we are certainly on alert. If something special turns up we will not turn it down, but we are not desperate because we have a big depth in our squad." A confident assertion, but one that flew in the face of the reality. Arsenal were heavily reliant on individual players remaining fit and in form in too many positions for their own good.

Chapter 3

Hope or Expectation?

"The owner, directors, chief executive and manager of Arsenal should all hang their heads in shame. Collectively culpable." This damning criticism by Tim Payton, the chief spokesperson of the Arsenal Supporters' Trust, came in response to the 3-1 opening day Premier League home defeat to Aston Villa. Such a woeful performance had brought about a dramatic change of view; Payton had previously been urging patience on his Twitter account with regard to the lack of reinforcements throughout the summer, believing club insiders who had briefed him that a major signing was imminent. However, nothing had happened by the day of the Villa defeat, and the *sangfroid* had evaporated. Payton was taken to task by one of the Trust members, Chris Hudson, for his summer tweets in a post-match interview with unofficial website *Arsenal Fan TV*, in which he expressed the same post-match sentiments as Payton, albeit with a liberal dose of industrial language:

"What you saw there was total incompetence by the board and the manager. It couldn't have gone any worse. They've had 90 days to buy players.

And I've got a message for Tim Payton and John Cross [the *Daily Mirror*'s Arsenal correspondent] and all you media luvvies – get off your arse and start saying it as it is. And the message to the board – either f***ing shape up or get out because you've let all the fans down.

You can't have £180 million in the bank and you're playing Cazorla, who just got off the plane from Ecuador [after representing Spain in a friendly international], and people are booing him because he's made a mistake. The reason he made the mistake was because he shouldn't have been on the pitch in the first place, because he's knackered. What is going on at this club?"

Hudson's articulate and heartfelt rant so captured the feeling of the moment that it became a viral sensation and garnered 750,000 hits within days of its posting on YouTube. And any sense of complacency regarding the lack of transfer activity was removed in one fell swoop. A case of "buy no one, get 1-3". A most inauspicious start to a season which, if it continued as it had begun, would constitue one of the longest periods that Arsenal had existed without a trophy.

That 17th August defeat exploded the lid off the pressure cooker of frustration at the club's lack of summer transfer activity and provided a focal point for the widespread dismay and disgruntlement amongst the supporters. The reality of the match in which Arsenal took an early lead through Olivier Giroud was that they were undone by some questionable officiating, including the award of a contentious penalty to go behind 2-1. The harsh dismissal of Laurent Koscielny for two yellow cards compounded the sense of injustice, as well as severely handicapping the team's chances of getting back into the game. Nevertheless, the selection of Jack Wilshere and Aaron Ramsey as the holding midfield pair (Mikel Arteta was injured) – two players more renowned for their attacking instincts than their defensive ability – showed up the paucity in the depth of the squad with no obvious conservative alternatives.

Arsène Wenger was barracked for not having purchased any new players, with the only arrival up to that point having been the immature striking prospect, Yaya Sanogo. The exasperation was perfectly expressed by the fans leaving the stadium in a series of post-match interviews for *Arsenal Fan TV*, including the aforementioned offering from Chris Hudson. Another supporter surmised: "In life you get what you pay for… unless you're an Arsenal fan." This thought was echoed by the former Liverpool player-turned-Sky Sports pundit Jamie Carragher, who stated: "The only people who are overspending at Arsenal are the fans." Even with 11 men on the field, the team had looked vulnerable in direct contrast to the previously undefeated ten Premier League matches that, less than four months ago, had secured a fourth place finish and another opportunity in Europe's showpiece club competition. With a visit to Istanbul for the first leg of the Champions League qualifier against the Turkish champions, Fenerbahce, only four days after the Villa game, the chances of making the lucrative group stage looked delicately balanced.

But one month later and Arsenal – following five successive victories, including two against Fenerbahce to secure their Champions League bounty for the sixteenth consecutive season – sat proudly on top of the Premier League table after a 3-1 victory against Sunderland at the Stadium of Light on 14th September, a run which also included a two-week hiatus for World Cup qualifying matches. Already safely tucked away were maximum points by the same score against Fulham at Craven Cottage and a hard-fought but deserved 1-0 victory at the Emirates against Tottenham.

The win in the north east was notable because it featured the effervescent debut of the club's £42.5 million record signing Mesut Ozil from Real Madrid. Ozil's performance, specifically his assist for the opening goal scored by Olivier Giroud, lived up to the pre-match hype. The German international controlled an aerial ball played forward to him with one touch, and with his second rolled a pass into the penalty area for the onrushing Giroud to strike first time. His debut goal followed just over a fortnight later in a home Champions League group victory against Napoli when he volleyed an Aaron Ramsey cross into the net.

There was no doubt that Ozil had established an immediate rapport with his colleagues and seemed well suited to his new team's possession strategy, even if the physical challenges and hectic pace of Premier League encounters saw him drift away from the action from time to time. The same accusation was levied at Dennis Bergkamp when he first arrived, which puts it into perspective. With gifted playmakers like Bergkamp and Ozil, the value comes from the crucial moments of insight such as a pass, on the face of it out of nowhere, to set up a goalscoring opportunity for a colleague. The Dutch master explained the prerequisite quick thinking and instant control: "The basic [thing] for me is the first touch. The first touch is so important. If you talk about Ozil, people say he is not marked properly, he always has a lot of space. But he has got that space because he can create space with his vision and his first touch. With that you create your own time." Ozil's exceptional skill not only created space for himself, but his precise passing created the same effect for his teammates, culminating in an ominous attacking midfield force whether his partners were Ramsey, Rosicky, Cazorla or Wilshere. "The timing of his passes and incisiveness," commented Arsène Wenger, "means we can turn from defence to offence very quickly."

Raised in Gelsenkirchen, Ozil, whose grandparents were Turkish immigrants, played his early football in a contained space that was known as the 'monkey cage' (*Affenkafig*), a fenced-in five-a-side pitch. Ozil explained how he had benefited from such unfriendly conditions: "The good thing with these cages is the ball never goes out and so the game goes on and on. The surface was rough, there were stones and it really hurt when you fell. It partly shaped the way I play. Most of the time I played against older kids so that shaped me too." He joined the local *Bundesliga* club, Schalke, and made his debut in 2006 at the age of 17, before moving to Werder Bremen two years later, where he won the German cup in 2009 by scoring the winner against Bayer Leverkusen. The same year, he had an influential role in the under-21 European Championships, culminating in the final when Germany demolished England 4-0. Before he was transferred to Real Madrid after his impressive 2010 World Cup – he was one of the main reasons why Germany trounced England 4-1 in Bloemfontein – Arsène Wenger had contemplated buying him, as Ozil revealed after eventually joining Arsenal three years later: "I had long conversations with Wenger before I joined Real," he recalled, "and that's how I got to know about Arsenal and the way they like to sign talented players who can move the ball well." However, in 2010 the reality was, as Ozil himself admitted: "When the offer came in to join Real Madrid, there is no decision to make. Let's be honest – you don't refuse this club."

Three seasons on, and once Real had decided that Ozil was expendable, with Wenger's obsession with possession play the move to north London appeared to be mutually beneficial for both manager and player. From first pulling on the red and white shirt, Ozil rarely gave the ball away and always looked to be able to create time and space even in the frenzied atmosphere of Premier League football. He assimilated the demand to live up to his billing with ease. After all, he had just arrived after three years at Real under Jose Mourinho, where he won the Spanish cup (*Copa del Rey*) in his first season and the league title in his second. He described the intense atmosphere of his time in Madrid: "The pressure is so huge because you have to go and really win absolutely every game. There is no game where people don't expect you to win. So having played there for three years, pressure is nothing that would scare me... I love playing football. So I go out to play and I don't really feel pressure. Of course, there are some days when things just don't work out as well as they do on other days, but that doesn't have anything to do with pressure."

Although nominally positioned as the advanced central midfielder operating in the space behind the main striker, Ozil had no problems in coming to terms with the fluidity required at his new club: "The manager wants us to move around and swap positions," he confirmed. "Sometimes I move over to the flank and then Cazorla is in the central position, sometimes it's Rosicky. It makes it harder for the opposition to stop us. Of course I am happy to play in the playmaker position because I have my freedom there. But you have to make spontaneous decisions on the pitch. When you notice gaps you move over to the left or to the right. You have to find space. That's why I'm sometimes found on the wing. I play the same way in the national team. It's one reason – that we change positions – why we [Germany] are so successful and score so many goals."

The winning run continued at home against Stoke City (3-1) and in Wales against Swansea (2-1), and thereby ensured that the leadership was retained going into October. In Europe, the same positive results were attained in Marseilles (2-1) and at home to Napoli (2-0), which put Arsenal in pole position in their Champions League group; a total of eight successive conquests. In fact, taking into account the climax to the 2012/13 season, the team had created a club record for the most consecutive away victories, ten in total.

However, all good things have to come to an end, and it was ironically third time unlucky for the trip to the Hawthorns in early October where the two previous visits had culminated in a fortunate maximum six points, without which Champions League qualifications would not have been obtained in 2012 and 2013. After five successive Premier League wins, the 1-1 draw against West Bromwich Albion meant that Arsenal had taken 16 points out of a possible 21. Though, to put the excellent return into some perspective, against the same opponents in 2012/13 they took the maximum points, 21 out of 21. (The pattern of the previous season's results continued in the next fixture with a win over Norwich City to make the comparative 2013/14 return of 19 points out of 24.) The sequence reflected the vagaries of the draw regarding Arsenal's 2013/14 fixture list, enabling them to top the table despite being – comparatively – five points worse off against the same opposition than in the previous campaign. The compelling conclusion was that the excellent start, after the first day's setback, was more a case of Wenger's boys only doing what was expected of them and beating the teams they should do, although of course the run of consecutive wins on their travels was a healthy habit to adopt whatever the circumstances.

In the seven weeks from the start of the season on 17th August, Arsenal had played 11 matches and, perhaps, the number of games took their toll on the squad because of the inability to ring the changes in certain positions. Arsène Wenger had restricted his freedom to choose by his conviction that an 18-man squad should be the foundation of his selection policy. Certainly, if his players were talented enough, versatile and remained free from injuries, then the policy should have been vindicated. On the other hand, with the history of injuries and suspensions, it seemed to be tempting fate not to have added to both the quality and quantity of the squad in the summer. In fact, in the last two transfer windows, January and summer 2013, Arsenal had spent money on only one undisputed first-team member, Mesut Ozil. They also paid £8.5 million for Nacho Monreal as full-back cover (and both Yaya Sanogo and Mathieu Flamini arrived on free transfers).

As the 2013/14 season progressed, the side appeared more composed and able to head off danger in an efficient, disciplined manner, maintaining the good defensive habits acquired during the successful run to the end of the previous season. Ozil's arrival was undoubtedly a catalyst to the positive feeling around the place, enhanced by the triumphant sequence of victories, but fingers were crossed that the top and tail of the team – goalkeeper Szczesny, the two central defenders Mertesacker and Koscielny (the midfield was well stocked with both defensive and attacking options), and above all, as the sole striker, Giroud – would not suffer injury or suspension.

In hindsight, perhaps the Villa result served to shock the club out of any sense of complacency as to what the supporters were willing to tolerate in the light of a total lack of spending in the transfer market with only a couple of weeks remaining to alter the status quo. The subsequent victorious run raised confidence and expectations, but the caveat remained that, apart from Tottenham, none of Arsenal's main rivals had been faced. With Liverpool and Manchester United on the horizon, the AGM would be held before the resumption of hostilities at the end of October after another international break.

Chapter 4

Money – That's What I Want

"I want to make this club the biggest club in the world," Arsène Wenger told a marketing acquaintance before the move to the new stadium in 2006.

"OK, but you can't," was the response.

"I will."

"No, it's impossible, there are three key sources of income – matchday, commercial and television – and Manchester United will always be a bigger a business, a bigger brand than Arsenal."

"I don't think so."

"Well your heart is talking, not your head."

"My head is talking," insisted Wenger. "I think that if we achieve the 60,000 stadium, we will make more gate money than Manchester United."

"That is true, but you have tremendous investment to claw back."

"Exactly, but you know I came here to bring my football way of thinking to this club, to win things and as well to make this club step by step bigger."

The ability to generate revenue is the path to success for every football club. The more you earn, the more you can spend on acquiring the best players who reward you with titles, trophies and commercial growth; a successful team is the source of a successful business. A truly virtuous circle.

Far from challenging Manchester United since the move to the Emirates in 2006, Arsenal have been overtaken by United's 'noisy neighbours'. A combination of Abu Dhabi investment, together with the enormous fees Etihad Airways have paid to sponsor the stadium, the training centre and the shirt, have seen Manchester City's 2013 turnover triple to £271 million since Sheikh Mansour became the owner in 2008, poised to overtake Arsenal (£280 million).

And yet, even if it wasn't his direct responsibility, Arsène Wenger's boast was not entirely spurious. Although he would inevitably have fallen short of his objectives, had he and his colleagues appreciated the true value of their brand earlier than they did then Arsenal could have mounted a stronger commercial challenge. Whilst the move to the Emirates and the annual qualification for the Champions League had seen phenomenal increases in matchday (gate receipts, season tickets, corporate hospitality, programmes and catering) and broadcast revenue, the club has failed to realise its full commercial potential (the stadium and kit sponsorship, kit supply and merchandising, advertising, tours and tournaments, events and social media). Alisher Usmanov was right on the money when he opined in July 2013: "I think there are also many questions about the [effectiveness] of the commercial management at Arsenal, but we will see and we will wait. Maybe when I wake up someday, I will help the Arsenal club." In the meantime, despite the lack of a sugar daddy, Arsenal should be able to face the future with confidence if they exploit their brand values to the full and thus fulfil their commercial potential.

By and large, sports fans detest the description of the game they love as a 'product' or the club that is a centrepiece of their lives as a 'brand'. Whilst they have some justification for their dismissive view of the former, they are perhaps not fully conversant with the importance and the power of the latter. A product is produced in a factory, but a brand is created in the mind, imbued with both rational and emotional values. Most people tend to think of brands as commercial products with their specific logos and well-established names. They think of supermarket goods and other advertised and promoted products, such as consumer durables ranging from cars to electronic equipment. Brands in these product categories, and indeed all brands, share a set of attributes and experiences that enables them to create their own identity, their own personality and distinguish themselves from competitors – the name, the packaging, the price, the selling process, how its representatives behave and what response the total mix generates, particularly nowadays through social media. So any product, service or person who can establish their own set of values and represent them by their own trademark, badge or logo can be a brand.

So all football clubs are brands in their own right. More than that, they have certain qualities that mark them out as special. They are part of the supporters' daily existence, adding colour and excitement to their lives. They provide a common reference point for likeminded souls and, most important, the dramatic nature of the game holds supporters in thrall and provides magic moments whether you are supporting Accrington Stanley or Arsenal. Thus, in order to produce the optimum business, Arsenal must appreciate the unique qualities of its brand and play the hand it has created for itself.

The name 'The Arsenal', the cannon, the crest with the Latin motto *Victoria Concordia Crescit* (victory develops through harmony), the red shirts with white sleeves, Highbury and, to a lesser extent, the Emirates,[3] are all distinctive elements of the Arsenal brand. They provide recognition of the values that have made the brand powerful: the history and tradition created by dominant personalities such as Sir Henry Norris, Herbert Chapman, George Graham and Arsène Wenger, and the great players from Cliff Bastin to Thierry Henry and the 'Invincibles' of 2003/4 who brought pioneering on-field success. Off the field the exploits of these legends were supervised and supported by generations of long service personnel, such as the patriarchal families of the Bracewell-Smiths and the Hill-Woods. The sum of a number of very important diverse parts working together to make up a unique and special phenomenon: the Arsenal brand. Brands are also defined by comparison to what they are not. Cadbury's is not Mars, Waitrose is not Sainsbury's, and Arsenal is definitely not Tottenham Hotspur or Manchester United.

Unlike Manchester United, whose former commercial development director, Ben Hatton, claimed, "We [Manchester United] are a business first and foremost ... we're not just into the football business.' On the other hand, Arsenal, according to Ivan Gazidis, are first and foremost a football club: "Ultimately, this is a football club, and a club in any non-technical

---

[3] Whilst Highbury could claim to be 'the home of football' and be synonymous with the club – Arsenal is Highbury and Highbury is Arsenal – the Emirates has replaced Highbury as Arsenal's home. However, as a result of the extraneous sponsorship the stadium will never have the same intrinsic contribution to the Arsenal brand as Highbury.

sense of the word is owned by its fans because without fans the club doesn't exist." (The short-term property sideline notwith-standing – principally the construction and sales of 650 luxury apartments, Highbury Square, on the site of their old stadium – the directors viewing it as an opportunity too good to pass up, the sole objective of which was and is to provide revenue to be used by the football club. The Arsenal Supporters' Trust has estimated that £60 million has been accrued from the property side of the business.)

There is probably no other area of commercial life where loyalty is so ingrained as football. Even at the worst of times – successive relegations, ignorant owners who wish to move away from inherent principles such as the team colours or even the name of the club itself – it is the fans who maintain the sense of identity and, whether they consciously realise it or not, are the true custodians of the brand ("Love the team, hate the club" becomes a rallying cry when the board/man-ager get it disastrously wrong).

In the dominant USA sports – gridiron football, baseball, bas-ketball and ice hockey – the ruling body exercises central control over its constituents' members. Thus, whilst the Dallas Cowboys is an important brand in its own right, it is wholly subservient to the National Football League (NFL) brand. The draft system is the cornerstone of the sport. It is the only way that players are acquired and is controlled in such a way that the first pick of college graduates – the only way new recruits enter the profes-sional game – is given to the bottom team, thereby preventing dynasties so that today's champions often become tomorrow's also-rans. Together with the provision of a salary cap and equal sharing of commercial income, the regulations ensure that the competitive balance of the league is maintained.

In England, the reverse holds true. What holds sway in the Premier League are the big clubs who create the momentum and drive the league. It is not Southampton versus Aston Villa that attracts the highest ratings in the UK or across the world but the top clubs – Manchester United, Arsenal, Chelsea, Manchester City and Liverpool – the dominant forces of the Premier League, particularly when they play against each other. So keen is the rivalry and so attractive the contests, that it is quite likely, largely as a consequence of the latest broadcast deals, that by 2016 there will be more than half a dozen English clubs in the top twenty richest football clubs in the world.

So it is the international brands who, in football just as in the commercial world, set the agenda and dominate the landscape because of their triumphs, history, wealth and earning capacity. The Premier League, due to the indolence of the Football Association (FA), has long ago disappeared over the horizon with all of the hype and all of the money, the chief beneficiaries of which are the top clubs. (And for this select few of the privileged Premier League members' club, there is the added treasure trove from also being admitted to the inner sanctum of the Champions League.) As a consequence of the succession of lucrative broadcasting contracts since its inception, primarily courtesy of Sky Television, the Premier League has grown to become an omnipresent global force. Televised in over 200 countries, it is the most popular club competition and thus rivals the NFL as the richest sports league in the world.

Paradoxically, since the move to the new stadium, which was intended to make Arsenal a financial powerhouse, Arsenal's position amongst the elite of the elite of domestic clubs has been first threatened, and in the last couple of years usurped by the free spending of initially Chelsea and then Manchester City. Nonetheless, whilst only Manchester United, Barcelona and Real Madrid generate more matchday income than Arsenal, and the latest domestic and overseas broadcast deal which commenced in 2014 should deliver an additional £40 million for a top four English club and a similar sum from a successful Champions League campaign, Arsenal's commercial income is far less than that earned by any other leading club, at home or abroad.

The long-standing agreements with Emirates and Nike have been the major cause of Arsenal's comparative weakness, their hands being tied by the timing and the length of the contracts, of necessity agreed to facilitate funding for the new stadium whilst in the meantime market values have soared. Only belatedly in 2014 did a new Emirates shirt sponsorship agreement extend the relationship to 2019 at £30 million per annum (though as part of the deal, the airline will also continue to give its name to the stadium until 2028). And Puma paid a similar amount to replace Nike as the club's kit supplier from the start of the 2014/15 campaign. Both represent significant increases on the previous deals of shirt sponsorship (£6 million per annum) and kit supplier (£8 million per annum). So eventually the club has recovered some lost ground – Manchester United, Liverpool and Manchester City had already pocketed £25 million plus on both sponsorship and kit supply for a number of years – although arguably the main beneficiary is Emirates, who reap the rewards of their dual shirt and stadium sponsorship to such an extent that they have the highest sponsorship recognition of all Premier League clubs, with over 60 per cent of people questioned being aware of the partnership with Arsenal.

Once again, the example of Bayern Munich shows Arsenal how naming rights could have been used as part of a more profitable strategy. The German champions have a three-part agreement with long-term partners Adidas and Audi, recently joined by the insurance giant Allianz, who have given their name to the new stadium. All three companies have their head-quarters in Bavaria and have each taken an 8.3 per cent stake in the club, which not only makes them an integral part of the business but they paid handsomely for the privilege, jointly making their financial contribution more than double that of Emirates in north London. Moreover, no sooner had Arsenal patted themselves on the back on their incremental sponsor-ship deals than Manchester United stole their thunder by once again raising the bar in 2014. United anticipated a bidding war for their new shirt contract, with negotiations starting at twice the rate that Puma will pay Arsenal. And even this stupendous deal may not match the world record amount paid by United's new shirt sponsor in 2013. Although not appearing on the shirt until the start of the 2014/15 season, Chevrolet paid £12 million for the right to replace AON as part of a seven-year sponsorship deal worth $559 million (£357 million).

So what can Arsenal do to improve their commercial per-formance and increase their commercial revenue? A starting point would be to recognise that going hand in hand with the development of brand values must be an appreciation of the Arsenal brand as a sponsorship medium, and an attractive one in its own right. The core audience of football support-ers in general are young, free-spending males, who are light television viewers and therefore notoriously difficult to reach through the usual paid-for advertising channels. They can be numbered in millions across the world and therefore football offers a cost-effective way of promoting products and services such as alcohol, mobile technology, financial services and cars.

Further, a close association with the club provides the added advantage of the endorsement of a respected patron and the facility to tap into a loyal fanbase. Thus, since 2012 a concerted effort by the commercial department under Tom Fox has produced a range of regional partners to supplement half a dozen official partners (Carlsberg, Citroen, Gatorade, Huawei (smartphones), Indesit and Jean Richard watches). Traversing the continents from Africa – a summer 2013 trip to Nigeria sponsored by the regional Guinness company was cancelled due to last-minute financial and security issues – through India to the Far East, these new affiliates are testimony to both Arsenal's global appeal and the development of social media. Indeed, the ability to add partners, at least on a regional basis, appears infinite, though it would be enhancing for Arsenal to have some more global brands in their portfolio.[4]

Of course, whilst there is a maximum number of 60,000 people who can be accommodated in the stadium, there is no limit to the number of potential Arsenal fans on a worldwide basis (estimated in 2014 to number around 50 million). Whilst the majority of these men, women and children may never see the team in the flesh, apart from the pre-season Asian tours, whose scarcity make them so popular and lucrative, supporting the team by television and social media does not make them lesser fans, merely different. However, the youthful majority are probably not willing to endure a consistent fall in their expectations, which is exemplified by the staggering number of 'unlikes' (450,000) Manchester United's Facebook page received after their 3-0 home loss to Liverpool in March 2014. On the other

---

[4] A persuasive new business presentation which faithfully extols the values of the brand has been helpful in this respect, the only drawback being, excellent though he is, the use of Arsène Wenger as a spokesperson underplays his fundamental role in the creation and representation of the brand itself.

hand, having broken their trophy duck Arsenal could envisage a terrific impetus for their business.

For most fans of a certain age, like John Simmons, Arsenal was an inherited love. As he explained in an email to his son, Matt, recorded in their ground-breaking book, *Winning Together: The Story of the Arsenal Brand*: "Many people will be shocked, or think I'm being frivolous, when I say that the thing that I was always keenest to pass on to you was a love of the Arsenal. But that's the truth. I'm sure it was the same for my father. And the fact that your sister, Jessie, is Arsenal through and through doubles my delight and relief." Obviously this homespun indoctrination is not applicable in China, Malaysia or Indonesia, but being domiciled overseas does not automatically signify second-class fan status. The foreign fans show their support in the only ways that are open to them: buying the merchandise, subscribing to Premier League football and increasingly using social media. The intensity of feeling at its most extreme was demonstrated by stories from Kenya, such as an Arsenal fan stabbing a Liverpool fan after the pair watched the 5-1 defeat of the Gunners in February 2014, and another who committed suicide after Arsenal were eliminated by Manchester United in the Champions League semi-final in 2009. The paradox facing Arsenal is that, while the majority of their income comes from domestic sources (and the Champions League), they have a global fanbase. The challenge facing the club, and indeed all superclubs, is how to transform this worldwide audience into worldwide customers.

All the same, facing up to this challenge does not mean deserting the parochial roots of north London (though in the minds of some die-hard Tottenham fans, even after all this time, Arsenal are still regarded as 'sarf' London interlopers from Woolwich). Identification begins at a local level and the relationship that Arsenal has with the borough of Islington and the local community has been for many years a key constituent of the brand. That's why the move to the new stadium, a few hundred yards down the road, was so important. The directors understood, protected and maintained the local links and ignored the temptations of a much easier and more economical build on the outskirts of London. Indeed, the largely unheralded 'Arsenal in the Community' programme has for over 25 years – for much of the time under the considerate and watchful eye of Alan Sefton – with a plethora of education and training schemes, been a terrific force for good. So much so that in the autumn of 2013, the council were able to mount an exhibition proudly 'Celebrating 100 Years of Arsenal Football Club in Islington'. The social responsibility and good deeds provide a much-needed empathetic human face, which counterbalances the unfortunate overriding necessity of the excessive money making schemes which are an unavoidable fact of life for all major football clubs.

Thus, it is no surprise that Arsenal have prioritised social media in order to extend the reach and the appeal of their business, executing a highly successful strategy. Social media has grown exponentially in recent years and has become a vital tool in driving consumer conversation and building engagement with the club. In November 2013, Arsenal attained the astounding number of 3 million followers on Twitter, at the time the most of any British sports team and the fifth largest in the world after Barcelona, Real Madrid, LA Lakers and Galatasaray. What has stimulated Arsenal's momentum is the very open approach they have, evidenced by the live posting of player tweets on the official Arsenal website.

Until recently, football fans were restricted in their access to the objects of their affections. The clubs did not know how to capitalise on their commitment and were wary of their involvement beyond the subservient role of paying customer. The prevalence of social media has broken down this barrier and has now become a necessary form of dialogue between the club and its audience, allowing a connection with the team for those unable to afford the cost of stadium attendance. This is significant in the light of Arsenal, already the most expensive team to watch in the UK, with season ticket prices for 2014/15 having risen by 3 per cent. Free social media at least goes some way to keeping the financially and physically (due to geographical distance) less able supporters in the loop.

Social media platforms such as Facebook and Twitter have revolutionised the way the fans are able to involve themselves with football. Whether it is just to receive the most up-to-date information, debate the latest controversy with other supporters or find out what the supposed experts have to say, they have been the impetus behind a new social media strategy to expand the boundaries of the brand, such as communicating a plethora of exclusive content, including player interviews, competitions and behind-the-scenes videos and photos, often presented with a degree of humour and lack of pretentiousness.

The use of 'hashtagging' plays a pivotal role in allowing clubs to funnel social media conversations into a single controllable stream. For this reason, Arsenal have used a bespoke hashtag for each game or special event (such as the unveiling of the Dennis Bergkamp statue in Feb 2014 – #DB10Statue), prompting their worldwide fanbase to interact with each other and adding another layer to the overall fan experience. The 2013 summer signing of Mesut Ozil led to the creation of the hashtag #OzilIsAGunner to channel conversations about their star signing onto a single stream on social media. The club-generated hashtag was used over 200,000 times, while the club also boasted an increase in Twitter followers of just under 70,000 in a week. (The increase in traffic on their associated streams further enhanced Arsenal's reach as a medium and their attractiveness to potential partners.)

Presented with the opportunity to interact directly with a favourite player can be the fulfilment of a dream for both young and old alike. Fans are encouraged to tweet anything on their mind and the best questions will get answered, subject to filtering out any unacceptably controversial or embarrassing issues. Nevertheless, it is both refreshing and brave that the club has encouraged a dialogue with the two sets of people who really matter – the players and the fans. Discovering which video games team members play, what their favourite television programme or film is, or what music they listen to, creates personal interactions and cements the sense of identity and affinity between the club and its supporters.

And the availability of Instagram, a visual content sharing website, has also provided the fans with a vast number of personal images of the club and its players. The adage that 'a picture is worth a thousand words' has never been more true, providing access to a hitherto secret world. Arsenal has frequently uploaded photos from inside the dressing room or from training sessions and these intimate glimpses have raised the levels of interest around forthcoming events. Photos are also distributed by the official club photographer, Stuart MacFarlane, via his account on the popular photo-sharing website Flickr.

The obvious next stage is to actually try and follow the trailblazing American examples where social media activity has been monetised. For example, the NBA has aligned itself with Twitter in order to provide fans with live video and replay highlights. These real-time clips and replays are packaged in sponsorship tweets, where the sponsor content can be overlaid on the video or a select message can be transmitted beforehand. Such activity across social media will inevitably lead to more social media clauses incorporated in sponsorship deals, and subsequently many more promoted tweets on matchdays involving the clubs' partners and associates. Whether using public transport or sitting in a cafe, bar or restaurant, the convenience of Wi-Fi is taken for granted. Yet, it is virtually non-existent in most UK football stadia.

San Francisco 49ers' new stadium – Levi's Stadium – serves as a model for new stadiums in every sport. Scheduled for completion in time for the 2014/15 NFL season, it is to be equipped with the best publicly accessible Wi-Fi network, which can support a packed house full of smartphone-wielding fans (capacity 68,500). They will be able to download a 49ers app that allows them to find the shortest beer or toilet queues, while also providing them with the ability to access live, in-game video, including the official television feed with a 30-second rewind feature for replays and the ability to switch from various camera angles.

Real Madrid and Barcelona were the first clubs in Europe to recognise the enhanced commercial possibilities by installing Wi-Fi in the Bernabeu and the Nou Camp in 2012. The Emirates only needs to look as far as Manchester to see how the Etihad has been transformed into the Premier League's most technologically fan-friendly stadium. City fans are able to surf the web on their smartphones and share their live match experiences on a worldwide basis via the social media platforms.

In the near future, the Etihad will offer live video which could incorporate content such as highlights from multiple angles, just as Sky Sports do in their coverage.

From a commercial point of view, a connected stadium would facilitate sponsorship tie-ups, in-play betting and e-commerce. And in addition to the income, the usage could potentially provide the club with important data which would offer information on attitudes and behaviour, and therefore allow for example advertisements or promotions to be demographically tailored and sent directly to a fan's smartphone.

A few years ago BW (Before Wenger), similar demographic information could be ascertained, but it required an appreciation of, and commitment to, market research. The Arsenal vice-chairman, David Dein, phoned a friend in an advertising agency to ask if he could recommend a research company. "That's terrific," said his friend, astonished at the nature of the request. "You're actually going to find out what the fans want."

Sometime later the ad man spoke to the research company, who revealed that Dein had asked them to design a questionnaire for the matchday programme. Embarrassed, he immediately phoned Dein and expostulated: "I gave you the recommendation in good faith. I thought you were going to do a quantified study. A questionnaire in the programme is a cop-out. It's not proper research. All you'll get is selective, contaminated information from a restricted, biased sample. It won't help you at all and the results may even mislead you."

Unsurprisingly, the observations were ignored (the Arsenal commercial department at the time comprised Dein, two chiefs, a few Indians and Stan the warehouseman), but the project proceeded and Arsenal felt that they were better informed about the needs and wants of their fans. Perhaps it was no coincidence that the subsequent launch of the North Bank all-seater stand at Highbury was an initial PR disaster.

Having decided on a controversial course of action to finance the new development – fans who had previously stood on the North Bank terrace would now have to pay for a bond of either £1,100 or £1,500 for the right to buy a season ticket seat – the publicity provoked such a hostile reaction that the club failed to sell anything like the number of bonds they hoped for. Many supporters were simply able to buy a seat on a match-by-match basis, albeit for a much higher price than they were previously asked to pay for standing.

Times have changed for the better and the willingness of Tom Fox and his 100+ colleagues in Arsenal's commercial department to embrace modern marketing methods has paid handsome dividends. Strategy is now far more considered, with a view to the long term rather than making a quick buck. Arsenal's recognition of the importance of using modern technology to reach as many people as possible is shown by the decision to make their online television platform, *Arsenal Player*, available free to anyone who registers an email address with the club. This information provides Arsenal (and their commercial partners if the registrant is willing) with the opportunity to communicate directly via email with the supporter concerned and, if they provide a phone number, by text message as well. Presumably it was decided that the benefits of being able to identify and target an increased number of supporters would far outweigh the immediate financial gains of retaining the service on a paid subscription basis.

Only one aspect of the available weapons remains off limits. The free publicity generated by the mass media for all top clubs has allowed them to believe that paid-for advertising is superfluous. Yet it is an integral component of all great brands, as vital as the name, product or service benefits, packaging and price, and therefore should be part of a football club's armoury. Indeed, Arsenal subscribe to the principle by using the players to model the kit in their matchday programme and monthly magazine, but they are only preaching to maybe a maximum of 50,000 of the already converted fanbase. Just imagine the sales impact of a television commercial featuring say Thierry Henry and Olivier Giroud extolling the virtues of the shirt and why obtaining one should be a badge of honour for all Arsenal fans.

Chapter 5

So Far, So Good

So farewell Peter, the last of the Hill-Wood dynasty which began in 1927. Not so fondly remembered for his sign-ing-off comment, "Thanks for your interest in our affairs" in winding up the 2012 AGM, the long-time Arsenal chairman (he took up the position after his father's death in 1982) was forced to step down from the board due to ill health after suffering a heart attack in December 2012. His final AGM had been an anti-climax, with an air of restlessness amongst many of the small shareholders at the direction the club was taking. Following the departure of Robin van Persie and the perception that the board continued to prioritise profits over trophies, the disquiet was exacerbated by the lack of activity in the transfer market and the abject performance in the first match of the 2013/14 season.

The departing chairman was replaced by a former colleague from Hambros Bank and Arsenal director, Sir Chips Keswick. Sir Chips confirmed the continuation of the 'us and them' approach when he presided over the AGM in October 2013, by stating that Stan Kroenke had fulfilled his obligation in his offer document (issued in 2011 when he purchased Danny Fiszman's shares and made a compulsory offer to buy those of every other shareholder) to meet with supporters' groups by just turning up and speaking for a few minutes at the annual gathering. In the patrician manner Sir Chips shared with his predecessor, he steered through the ritual formalities, engaging with the audience as little as possible. Even ardent loyalist Maria Petri (a long-time supporter, notorious amongst the fans for her resounding "Come on you Gunners" chant during matches) was hushed when she attempted to interject at a relevant point to inform the meeting that an Arsenal Ladies' game was being played that afternoon.

The tone of the meeting was in stark contrast to the last one, and was much more stage-managed so that there was little possibility for any ad hoc contributors to disrupt the meticulously planned proceedings. Pre-submitted questions appeared on a video screen with no opportunity for any follow up if the answers provided by Sir Chips or CEO Ivan Gazidis were unsatisfactory, which they were on occasion. This was unfortunate, as the subjects were all relevant. They ranged from the general (the ambitions of the club, the transfer policy, youth and commercial development) to the specific (the price of tickets, the composition of the board and the accountability of the manager). There was just time, as the clock ran down, for a handful of questions from the floor. These were most notable for Gazidis' response to the fact that maybe Tottenham were stealing a march in the USA when he admitted: "I'm aware of the Gareth Bale poster all over Times Square. But he doesn't play for Tottenham anymore. Now he plays for one of our rivals." Also when Sir Chips courteously sidestepped the issue of why Alisher Usmanov was not on the board.

Arsène Wenger gave his traditional speech, but no longer interacted with his audience by taking questions as he had in previous years. He outlined his strategy for a successful future, emphasising that "the core of the team has to be developed inside the club" and mentioned a number of first-team regulars to prove his point. He then stressed the importance of good coaching and scouting, although he admitted, "You don't need a scout to buy Mesut Ozil," adding, "I hope we have shown you we are not scared to spend." He continued by warning that, because of the extraordinary sums that were now coming into European football, competition would be even tougher in the future: "There used to be four or five clubs that could win the Champions League, now I could name ten because they have the budgets." All the same, he remained optimistic and ended by forecasting that, "I am confident we will all be happy in May."

Neither Wenger nor Ivan Gazidis trotted out the usual explanation that Arsenal would be in good shape when UEFA's obligatory Financial Fair Play arrived. Well, it had and Arsenal were. But there were no new commitments as a consequence. "Another healthy set of figures," as Peter Hill-Wood used to refer to past results, was announced, with a turnover of £280 million, a cash balance of £153 million, profits of £7 million and a significant increase in commercial revenues which can be expected to continue in 2014/15 – so no need to sell the best players in future, then.

Stan Kroenke expressed satisfaction with the continued progress, as he saw it, and stressed that there was no lack of ambition: "None of us up here – players, Arsène, board, fans – no one is happy until we have won championships and trophies," he said. If the owner truly craved the pleasure that a title or a trophy would bring, then why not invest in the enterprise? So far neither he nor the other directors had put money into the club, rather they had either sold or bought equity that has returned a handsome profit or multiplied in value respectively. Why not consider Alisher Usmanov's proposal, made on several occasions, for a share issue? Additional shares could be created which would, at a stroke, provide a very significant lump sum to enhance the manager's transfer and wages budget. Of course, such a move would dilute Stan Kroenke's holding, but not to such an extent that he couldn't safely hang on to his majority stake. More importantly, his club would be at least £100 million better off. Arsène would still not be able to stockpile talent, not that he would ever want to, in the manner of Manchester City's ten £20 million-plus signings, but he could boldly go head to head with them, or indeed any other club in the world, for *the* star he really wanted. The absence of any enthusiasm for the proposal was probably due to the directors' wish to keep Usmanov and his 30 per cent holding at arm's length and off the board. Any concession might entail paying more attention to his other ideas, which they feared might take the club in a direction they had no desire to follow, such as his view that the commercial strategies could be developed. The brusque initial putdown that Peter Hill-Wood dismissed Stan Kroenke's possible involvement in 2007 – "We don't want his sort and we don't want his money" – was perhaps a fair reflection of how the directors regarded the Uzbek billionaire in 2013.

In practice, for Arsenal to win the Premier League title, they would have to carry out Tony Adams' dictum of how to do it to the letter – take the maximum 60 points from the bottom ten clubs and allow for some slip-ups away from home against their main rivals. As the 2013/14 season progressed, the team duly set about doing just that, extending their early good form in the first post-AGM fixture by destroying Norwich with a scintillating display. Ozil's finesse was contagious and the double one-touch give-and-go combination between Wilshere and Giroud that led to the first goal in the 4-1 rout looked as if it might have been copied, play by play, from the Barcelona manual of winning with style. The three points put Arsenal two clear of Liverpool at the top of the table, a position that was maintained after a resilient 2-0 away victory against Crystal Palace, the second goal scored despite the visitors being reduced to ten men as a result of a red card for Mikel Arteta.

Sandwiched between the two league wins were two home cup defeats against Dortmund in the Champions League and Chelsea in the League Cup. The ability to put the rebuffs to one side, move on and treat the Premier League as a separate exercise enabled Arsenal to capitalise on the momentum which had been built up in the continuous search for the next three points. The positive frame of mind was just as well as Arsenal now faced, albeit at the Emirates, their stiffest domestic challenge so far against second-place Liverpool.

The Merseysiders, under Brendan Rodgers, had emerged as genuine title challengers, their solid start enhanced by the return of Luis Suarez from suspension. Of course, for Arsenal at their most effective, attack is the best form of defence, though with the unfortunate by-product of encouraging a tendency for being too casual in possession in their own half. Liverpool's equal lack of caution led to an ambitious, open encounter, the outcome of which looked to favour the team that created the most chances, and the hosts took enough of them to run out

2-0 winners. Mikel Arteta's post-match comment summed up his colleagues' state of mind when he said: "People have been waiting for us to lose. But we showed today the desire that we have to stay where we are [at the top of the league]."

So far, so good. Five points clear at the top of the table. Liverpool joined Tottenham as another tough home fixture safely negotiated, but the true test lay in the future: how would the team cope with the away encounters against their two vanquished foes and, more importantly, their closest rivals. Two of them awaited Arsenal in the next week, first up at the Westfalenstadion against Dortmund and then Old Trafford.

Wins are everything. They come from converting opportunities, which are few and far between at the pinnacle of international competition. Three weeks previously in London, Dortmund did precisely that and triumphed 2-1 in the third group fixture of the Champions League. In Germany, the boot was on the other foot. Another goal from the revelation of the season, Aaron Ramsey, extended Arsenal's sequence of European away wins which had begun in Munich with the pyrrhic victory against Bayern in the 2012/13 Champions League round of 16, six months previously. Having accused his players of being "naive" against Dortmund at home, Arsène Wenger now praised their common sense: "We looked more stable defensively because we have experience in midfield not to lose the ball in stupid positions. Dortmund are especially dangerous when you lose the ball, and to counter that, you need maturity." Trips to Germany obviously suited the Gunners, as they emerged unscathed from the toughest away test they had faced since that February night in the Allianz Arena, and with confidence and a self-belief that they had not taken to Manchester for some time.

However, back in Blighty it was the same old story. Another unbeaten run laid to rest at Old Trafford: this time it was the sequence of 15 away fixtures, while previously it had been the 'Invincibles" magnificent record of 49 games unbeaten. In mitigation, the visitors were not in the best of shape. Flu accounted for Mertesacker and Rosicky, and had left other members of the squad debilitated – though whether the absent defender would have prevented the United goal was open to question. One of the drawbacks of the zonal marking system favoured by Arsène Wenger is the inherent difficulty in tracking an opponent's run from a deep position outside the zone itself, which is how van Persie breached his former teammates' barricade. On the (big) assumption that everyone carries out the job allotted to them, man marking might be a better alternative at set pieces, though Arsenal probably didn't possess the personnel with sufficient defensive nous or discipline to see the system through and carry out the drill on a continuous basis.

There would not have been many Arsenal supporters perusing the fixture list at the beginning of the season who would have expected a different outcome, anticipating a futile struggle against the defiant defences, especially away from home, so the defeat to United wouldn't have surprised or disappointed them unduly. Besides the day could have been even more exasperating, but Manchester City lost away to Sunderland, Chelsea drew at home with West Brom and Tottenham lost at home to Newcastle.

The misfortunes of their rivals reaffirmed the necessity of resuming the winning sequence against the lesser teams right away, one of the best of whom, Southampton, was next in line at the Emirates. Although dominating – there were a couple of magic moments when Wilshere and Ramsey hit the woodwork

– Arsenal needed the assistance of the opposition goalkeeper, Artur Boruc (who gifted Olivier Giroud a goal after failing to deceive him with an overly ambitious attempt at a Cruyff turn), and the referee (who awarded a debatable penalty) to emerge 2-0 to the good.

With the prospect of seven games in the three weeks running up to Christmas, Arsène rang the changes for the penultimate Champions League group game against Marseilles: Monreal, Flamini and Rosicky replaced Gibbs, Arteta and Cazorla. With the distinct possibility that both Dortmund and Napoli could end up with 12 points – Marseilles had long since been cut adrift – no slip-ups could be afforded and Arsenal duly obliged with another 2-0 scoreline to take them to 12 points and probable qualification. The spine of Szczesny, Mertesacker, Flamini and Giroud, although somewhat light on flair, compensated with bags of commitment and were instrumental in forcing through the right result.

Keeping a consistent line-up was now a luxury due to the intensity of the fixture list. So, away to Cardiff on 30th November saw Flamini make way for Arteta, but his importance, and that of Walcott as well, was underlined when the pair entered the fray, the former to disturb Cardiff's rhythm and rally the troops, and the latter to provide an additional attacking outlet to give their opponents something to deal with. Both substitutes, with an element of role reversal, contributed to the two goals: Flamini scored a cracker, whilst Walcott set up Ramsey's second in a comfortable 3-0 win.

Until the visit to Wales, Olivier Giroud had started 20 of Arsenal's 22 competitive matches, missing only the two League Cup encounters in which Nicklas Bendtner replaced him. Fielding one central striker, who often had to plough a lone furrow, Arsène Wenger was overly dependent on the 27-year-old French international, prompting concern about what would happen if Giroud suffered an injury, fatigue or loss of form, and criticism that the squad did not possess enough depth to allow the striker more time off. Certainly, this was negligence that the manager had tacitly admitted to by his summer courting of Gonzalo Higuain and Luis Suarez, and the failed deadline day attempt to secure the loan of Demba Ba, the result of which was that Nicklas Bendtner remained at the Emirates instead of going to Crystal Palace.

Despite the fact that his own opportunities would have been affected if the attempts to hire new personnel had succeeded, even Giroud went as far as to admit, "It's necessary for the club to recruit another striker." However, he was enough of a pragmatist not to allow the circumstances to affect his attitude, asserting: "It's useless lamenting [the lack of] a high-profile signing. I know what I have to do and what I'm capable of. I'm focusing on me and my work. The coach is counting on me, so I don't think [about the situation] too much."

Olivier Giroud was signed by Arsenal from Montpellier for £13 million in 2012 after his French club won the *Ligue 1* Championship for the first time in their history. Giroud, with his 21 goals and nine assists, fulfilled a vital role which made him the league's top goalscorer and earned him a call-up to the national side. A late developer, aside from his two seasons with Montpellier, his professional career up until then had been spent in the lower echelons of the French league with Grenoble, Istres and Tours.

Initially because of his lack of top-class experience, Wenger probably considered his countryman to be more of a back-up for Robin van Persie rather than an automatic first-choice selection. In fact, however, Giroud joined in June 2012, about a month after van Persie had made it clear that he was not going to sign a new contract and that, as a consequence, it would just be a question of money and a matter of time before he was sold.

Even with van Persie out of the reckoning, Lukas Podolski started the early encounters of the 2012/13 campaign rather than Giroud. But as the weeks went by, the French international became the first choice for the centre-forward role, with Podolski either stationed out wide or relegated to the substitutes' bench. Given the demands of the lone spearhead role, Giroud appeared to be the better choice. Similar to the old-style centre-forward, good in the air and stronger and more combative than the smaller craftsmen who supported him, he reminded older fans of George Graham's favourite target man, Alan Smith, in the way that he held the ball up, brought his colleagues into play and finished off their moves. On the other hand, he was less clinical in front of goal than some of his notable predecessors and he certainly lacked the pace of Ian Wright and Thierry Henry. Further, he was guilty of squandering too many one-on-one chances and developed a reputation for only scoring infrequently outside the confines of the M25. Nevertheless, the return of 17 goals and 11 assists from his first Premier League season was a satisfactory initiation. And his improved strike rate in 2013/14 would buck the 'second season syndrome' trend – a reservation that pundits frequently cite to qualify a newcomer's successful introduction to the Premier League – especially in the big games, with clinical conversions in the Champions League.

Giroud's lack of ego also served him well: "I understand that Arsenal fans want a big name," he modestly said, "but I try to stay calm, to take it easy and concentrate on my job, train well, and repay the confidence of the boss. He always talks to me, trusts me – that's why he didn't buy another striker last summer and in January. I'm still here because the boss is pleased with my game, with what I can bring to the team. I know I'm not a player on the same level as someone like Suarez, but I know I can improve again. That's why I'm quite confident of my future here. This isn't a time to doubt myself. Sometimes a striker won't score for a month or two. It happens to every striker. But you've always got to believe in your quality and remember that people trust you." And the most important man in his professional life certainly did: "It's difficult up front," emphasised Arsène Wenger, "because every challenge he [Giroud] goes into is physical. He's not a guy who moves away from people to get the ball; he's a guy who fights with people to get the ball. When he comes out of the game, he has 50 fights behind him. That is more demanding than the guy who just runs away."

No one could argue with Giroud's application and work rate, ably demonstrated by his willingness to chase down goalkeepers and force errors which could lead to goals, such as the one at home to Southampton, but that very trait would inevitably take its physical toll. Towards the end of the 2013/14 campaign, Arsène Wenger reflected: "Maybe we should have rested him a bit earlier and given him a breather for a while. He played maybe too many games. He has gone through a more difficult period recently. It was a bit physical and mental as well with what happened to him." Wenger was referring to an embarrassing incident that made the front page of a Sunday tabloid when a kiss-and-tell model revealed that she had been in Giroud's hotel room in the early hours on the day of the Premier League match against Crystal Palace on 2nd February 2014. The player subsequently apologised, via Twitter, to "… my wife, family and friends and my manager, teammates and Arsenal fans," but his confession was not sufficient to spare him a fine and a demotion to the role of unused substitute in the critical knockout match against Bayern Munich. The fact that Wenger felt compelled to select the unproven Yaya Sanogo in his place for such an important game, not only confirmed how seriously he regarded the transgression, but revealed how his lack of activity in the transfer market had left him with no adequate alternative.

Wenger had come to depend on Giroud to such an extent that he was highly selective in choosing which matches to rest him for. As far as the Premier League was concerned, he only felt able to do this on the odd occasion when Arsenal were up against less challenging opponents at home during busier periods. So it was that four days after winning in Cardiff, Arsenal entertained Hull at the Emirates and, at last, Giroud could sit one out. He was replaced by Bendtner, who rewarded his manager and pleasantly surprised his numerous critics with a goal scored so early that a fair proportion of the crowd were not yet in their seats to see it. Perhaps the same fans also missed Ozil scoring shortly after the second half started. Well you pay your money and you take your choice. But with the exorbitant cost of tickets, the committed continue to be baffled that so many prioritise half-time food and drink (and an early departure) over the full 90 minutes.

Arsenal did enough to secure the points against Hull and little more, perhaps pacing themselves for the more rigorous tasks that lay in wait, the first of which was the visit of Everton. With a 1-1 draw the fair outcome from a tussle which either side could have emerged on top, the *Online Gooner*'s prescient assessment of the Merseysiders' credentials warranted careful note by Arsenal analysts: "After yesterday's match, at the very least, one has to consider Everton as a team that can take a top four place, come the season end. The fact that only one other side has managed to defeat them in the league – that being Manchester City at home – tells us that they have become harder to beat since David Moyes' departure. That they are only fifth is due to the large number of games they have drawn."

Both Chelsea and Manchester City had dropped points on their travels, which emphasised the importance of Arsenal's ability to win on theirs, in addition to the excellent home form, the combined effect of which by the second week in December was a five point lead at the top of the tree, in spite of the two dropped points against Everton. They now needed to maintain that pattern to overcome arguably the biggest obstacles in their path. To start, a trip to Naples for the final Champions League group game: the objective was to emerge as group winners and avoid the prospect of a more onerous tie that the runners-up position would invariably bring. The Italian job would be followed by a break of a mere three days before the team would undertake a shorter plane journey to Manchester, to face many people's favourite for the title. The spectre of City loomed large in Arsenal's thoughts, not just because they represented another potential Mancunian nemesis, but because of the manner of their achievements. As with Chelsea before them, their way of doing business annoyed Arsène Wenger – he termed it "financial doping" to emphasise what he felt was both clubs' unfair financial advantage. Even so, in his heart of hearts he could only approve of the way some of City's funds had been earmarked to lay the foundations of a state-of-the-art infrastructure that would not only benefit the first-team squad, but looking to the future would incorporate a long-term youth policy and community programme.

Arsenal were threatened by a City pincer movement, both in the short and long term: the omnipresent peril of the super-stars of today, while those of tomorrow were being groomed in the most auspicious environment. To add ironic insult to injury, Manchester City's youth programme was overseen by the 'Elite Development Squad Manager', one Patrick Vieira, an Arsenal legend, who reportedly had been willing to come back to the club he had adorned once he had hung up his boots as a City player in the summer of 2011. But the call never came.

In Vieira's symbolic absence, taken together with the lack of significant summer signings, the shareholders and supporters were left to ruminate on Stan Kroenke's implied commitment to obtain trophies, which he made at the AGM. But with millions still in the bank, they would have made a mental note to take the owner to task if the January transfer window saw a similar lack of action.

Chapter 6

THE BRADY BUNCH

"Arsenal is my club. They really looked after me when I was a kid – I came over at 15 – the people at the club and also the players. A lot of them were products of the [British] youth policy[5] – John Radford, George Armstrong, Frank Stapleton, Graham Rix, David O'Leary – that's why I say bringing a youngster through at Arsenal is in the DNA of the club." Liam Brady [6]

Over the two legs of the 2009 FA Youth Cup final against Liverpool, the victorious Arsenal side, managed by Steve Bould, utilised 17 players. Ideally the club would have liked to promote at least two or three of the group to the first-team squad, but up until the end of the 2013/14 season they haven't been able to do that. Less than five years after the Youth Cup triumph, the sale of Emmanuel Frimpong to Barnsley in January 2014 left only two of that successful squad on the club's books. One of those, Francis

---

[5] Before the 1990 Bosman ruling, which allowed freedom of movement throughout the European community, the youth policies of football league clubs were centred on the British Isles.

[6] Brady's quotes are taken from an interview with talkSPORT Radio in October 2012, unless otherwise stated.

Coquelin, had already been deemed surplus to requirements and spent the 2013/14 season on loan at *Bundesliga* club SC Freiburg. (Arsène Wenger even preferred to sign an injured 31-year-old midfielder, Kim Kallstrom, on loan for six months rather than recall Coquelin from Germany.) So it would appear that only Jack Wilshere was still part of the manager's plans.

Asked to recount the Academy (the club's in-house development programme for 9–18 year olds) successes, the director, Liam Brady, replied: "Certainly Ashley Cole. Still a great player and was a great player for Arsenal. He had only played seven or eight games [for the first team] and he was already an England international. He had that determination to succeed in abundance when he came to the club. We gave him a scholarship and then a pro [professional] contract." But Cole left the Academy over a decade ago and, in fact, when Brady arrived to take charge in 1996 he was fortunate to still find Cole there, his retention only due to the foresight of Brady's predecessor, Terry Murphy, and one of his long-serving scouts, Bill Hollingdale. As Hollingdale recalled in 2000, Cole started out as a striker, which the most talented boys usually did, but "[He] fell behind in terms of his height. It was touch and go whether he would be kept on and I remember Terry asking all the other coaches for their opinion. One by one they advised against retaining him. When Terry turned to me I told him I thought Ashley had a lovely touch. So Terry gave him another year and he hasn't looked back." (Murphy might also have been swayed by the persuasive pleading of Ashley's mother.)

Bringing the review up to date, Brady said: "Now at the moment [October 2012] we've got one of the best English players in Jack Wilshere. He's going to be a great player like Ashley. He's going to play an enormous amount of games for England. He is only going to get better."

Brady could have added Kieran Gibbs, although he only arrived after the abandonment of the Wimbledon youth scheme along with the transmogrification of the south Londoners into MK Dons. But notwithstanding the inclusion of Gibbs, the paucity of genuine graduates cannot be excused – Cole, Wilshere and Gibbs are the only really convincing instances of youngsters who have been developed by the Academy and gone on to make a decent first-team contribution.

When Brady said that developing youngsters was in the DNA of Arsenal, he was referring to the home grown British players of his and George Graham's era. For example, Tony Adams, David Hillier, Paul Davis, Michael Thomas, David Rocastle, Paul Merson and Kevin Campbell all earned a League Championship winning medal in 1991, and are probably the chief reason why the team is still so fondly remembered by supporters over the age of 30. These Englishmen fulfilled Johan Cruyff's mandatory qualification for an outstanding club side: "You need five, six, seven players from your own country," said the Dutch legend and former Barcelona coach. "The great teams at Madrid, Ajax, Milan, Barcelona, they all had that. It tells you something. You can have success, but to last there should be a [national] heart behind it."

Now the exception rather than the rule, the lack of English players is regretted particularly by the supporters nostalgic for the '91 side, along with many others. *La crème de la crème* of international superstars would always be welcomed anywhere, but the journeymen foreign players who block the path of young Englishmen are really only tolerated in a winning outfit. Hence the importance of growing your own who will eventually flourish in the first team, which, unfortunately, the Arsenal Academy has singularly failed to do. The very few successes out of the hundreds who have passed through the gates of the Hale End Academy in Walthamstow, East London raises legitimate questions as to what exactly is going on at the club. Is there an institutional failure at the academy level or simply a lack of willingness at the top to utilise its product?

Certainly, the infrastructure at Arsenal is in place and has been for over a decade. Speaking in 2003, Brady said: "The board has made a very substantial investment [at Hale End]. That compares [favourably] to training grounds that [other] Premiership clubs don't have. I've been to [Bayern] Munich and Ajax and we're all in the same park." And the right philosophy is evidently propounded. According to Brady: "You are looking for football intelligence, physical capabilities, drive and determination, and you are looking for skill. You don't often get all four [attributes] but when you do, you've got yourself a player." He elaborated: "You can improve technical ability with practice, but you've got to be learning the right things. And you can improve physically even at young ages. But I can't give a player football intelligence and you can't give them determination and courage to be able to handle the rigours of playing in front of 50,000 people." The recognition that some boys will never possess the right mental capacity was a constant obstacle that Brady faced, as he recalled back in 2003: "It is sad that some players are beyond shaping and advice and we lose a lot of talented players because they just haven't got the head for football, to realise it's more than just kicking a ball or running round the football field. It's the whole package. You bump into them later on and they say, 'I wish I had listened to you' but they won't listen at the time."

Not only has Brady had to cope with the growing pains of pubescent boys and willful teenagers, but he and his staff have had to come to terms with their Cinderella role in an imperfect system. With global domination the primary goal, the Premier League is no longer an English league but a cosmopolitan, international league that happens to be played in England. Certainly its success in terms of revenue and popularity is unquestioned and unrivalled. With a gap of £795 million over the German *Bundesliga*, the next wealthiest, the Premier League is the leading revenue-generating club competition in football. However, a country's football strength and standing cannot be measured by 20 clubs alone and, perhaps more importantly for the future, with a similar number of first-class academies. *Bundesliga* 1 and *Bundesliga* 2, the equivalent of the Premier League and Championship, give depth and resource to 36 clubs and an equal number of academies. Compared to the miniscule 3.5 per cent of the broadcast monies that the English Championship receives, *Bundesliga* 2 benefits from 21 per cent of their TV deal, which bridges the gap between the two divisions and allows other factors such as coaching and youth policies to have a propitious effect; money is not the paramount influence that it is in the Premier League.

The Premier League forced through the Elite Player Performance Plan (EPPP) in 2012 in an effort to come to terms with its self-imposed handicap when developing young English players (Roy Hodgson, the England manager, had fewer than 35 per cent of Premier League first teamers to select his 2014 World Cup squad from, compared to his compatriots in Germany, Spain and Italy, whose domestic leagues feature a majority of nationals).

The EPPP is a revolution that has radically changed the way that the top clubs acquire, coach and develop young players. The key bonus for these clubs is that EPPP increases the amount of time that their coaches can spend with their charges and, perhaps most importantly and most controversially, makes it much easier for the big clubs to sign teenage prospects from whomever and wherever they choose, from Football League and non-League clubs alike. Academies are graded 1 to 4, approximately reflecting the league status of the club they are attached to, on productivity rates, training, coaching, education and welfare facilities; the higher the grading, the greater the funding from the FA and the Premier League, but also the larger the initial investment. This ranges from £2.5 million at the top to £100,000 for a category 4 academy, which at first may appear equitable but is in fact unrealistic, the entry fees being loose change for the big clubs but beyond the pockets of many League Two outfits who have reluctantly been forced to shut down their youth programmes.

Another draconian change has seen the abolition of the tribunal system, which on occasions had sanctioned large up-front sums that were the elixir of life for the smaller clubs, such as the £700,000 down payment that Tottenham Hotspur were ordered to pay Crystal Palace for 16-year-old John Bostock in 2008 (and Palace felt they were shortchanged). Now there is an initial fee based on the grading of the academy, with subsequent payments depending on first-team appearances and England caps. Under the new rules, Palace, as an initial category 2 academy, would have been paid only £134,000, with Bostock unfortunately having failed to live up to expectations.

Once again the rules have been formulated in favour of the Premier League clubs, most of which enjoy category 1 status. The £500,000-plus fees paid for the likes of Bostock, and Luke Garbutt and Fabian Delph who Leeds sold to Everton and Aston Villa respectively, are the sort of sums (and in Delph's case, an astronomical £6 million) that smaller clubs will no longer receive; similar prospects will be snapped up much earlier and much more cheaply by the big clubs. In addition to the dramatic shortfall in the amount of compensation, the other major gripe of the Football League clubs is that the regulation on recruiting beyond the 90-minute journey radius for under-12s and an hour for under-16s was dropped, increasing the temptation for the kids (and their parents) at the smaller clubs to accept the ever-enticing offers from members of the Premier League. Further, anyone with a category 1 academy is free to visit the training grounds of the lower-ranked academies to run the rule over likely prospects. No wonder that Premier League scouts have reportedly had their cars damaged whilst casting their eyes over the boys of the lower league clubs.

In summary, EPPP can be cynically viewed as an unabashed manoeuvre by the Premier League in order to be able to cherry pick the best youngsters from the lower leagues. Lower-level clubs with an excellent track record of developing their own talent view the new regulation as nothing more than licensed larceny as they see their best prospects siphoned off for token remuneration. In their defence, the Premier League would like to convince the rest of the football community that their motives are altruistic, that EPPP will help the national team manager by increasing the pool of talent from which he can select. They add that if everyone is serious about improving the quality of young recruits, the elitist system will eventually raise standards across the entire professional game and not just at the very top. But a more prosaic interpretation would be that the policy merely facilitates compliance with UEFA's recent regulations regarding the number of 'home grown' players (a minimum of 8) that should be in their first-team squads for the professional leagues of the member associations. However, to comply with European Commission regulations, 'home grown' does not discriminate on the basis of nationality – the definition is any youngster, wherever he has come from, who has trained with his club for a period of three years between the ages of 16 and 21. So the Polish international Wojciech Szczesny, who joined Arsenal as a 16 year old, like other talented imports, was soon excused academy duties and placed in the senior youth or reserve squads in preparation for being dispatched on loan. In Szczesny's case, he went to Brentford as a 19 year old and soon became the first choice for the then League Two side. So the Polish goalkeeper would qualify as one of the obligatory quota, which is hardly going to help the prospects of first-team football for his English understudies; in Arsenal's case the problem is an academic one as they are all foreign anyway.

Arsène Wenger is fond of disclaiming that he never looks at the birth certificate of a wannabe, so, in effect, EPPP allows him *carte blanche* to raid other clubs both nationally and worldwide for teenagers with potential. Arsenal do not have to ensure that a certain number of academy entrants are English. Such a stipulation, however, does apply in Germany and it is therefore probably no coincidence that, since 2008, the national side has won the European Championships at under-17, under-19 and under-21 levels, and in so doing has created the most auspicious environment for supplying future senior internationals.

The 25-man rule has forced all the clubs to be more ruthless when deciding who shall stay and who shall go.[7] In Arsenal's

---

[7] Since 2011, all Premier League clubs have had to register a maximum squad of 25, which has to include eight home grown players, defined as those who have spent at least three years prior to their twenty-first birthday in a club's youth system. However, there is provision to supplement the squad with an unlimited number of players up to the age of 21, hence Arsenal's unusually large squad of 33.

case, this has caused them to release some young players earlier than they would have done in the past. Jay Emmanuel-Thomas, for example, despite demonstrating immense promise whilst coming through the ranks, was sold to Ipswich Town in 2011. At least Emmanuel-Thomas didn't suffer the fate of many of Arsenal's English contingent, who have found themselves watching on from the sidelines as more and more opportunities are given to their foreign contemporaries in the under-18 and under-21 teams. When these imports, like teenage German internationals Serge Gnabry and Gedion Zelalem, are brought in from abroad, they inadvertently provide insurmountable obstacles to their English colleagues hoping to make a breakthrough. Occasionally an ambitious youngster will notice the writing on the wall and jump ship. Nico Yennaris, a promising and highly regarded defender, made the difficult decision to leave Arsenal in 2014 for a new challenge at League One promotion candidates Brentford, where he at least enjoyed eight first-team outings in his debut season.

The Premier League has been only too pleased to have passed the hot potato of disciplinary measures involving their members to the FA. By the same token, it is the FA and not the Premier League who should be regulating EPPP for the benefit of the entire game, but, of course, money talks and the Premier League has most of it. Following their £5.7 billion broadcast deals from 2013–16, solidarity payments to the Football League were increased: each Championship club not subject to parachute payments received £2.3 million; League One clubs £360,000; and League Two clubs £240,000. And the parachute payments to the clubs relegated from the Premier League to the Championship, and in some cases beyond, was increased to £59 million over four seasons. The Football League also received substantial subsidies for youth development projects. The unspoken threat of the possibility of the withdrawal of these huge subsidies ensured that a majority of the Football League clubs, despite their reservations, voted for EPPP.

In the worst (financial) case scenario, it is small change for a top club to have to pay around £1.5 million for a prospect and to make provision for an annual academy budget of £2.5 million, of which up to a third could be provided by the authorities. The history of clubs such as West Ham, Aston Villa and Southampton, who provide a good coaching environment and a record of producing prospects who will have every chance of getting into the first team, should encourage their boys to stay. Regrettably, this state of affairs is not applicable to Arsenal.

Perhaps part of the answer lies in Liam Brady's explanation for entry and assessment criteria: "We don't place a lot of emphasis on results with our young age groups," he said. "It's all about bringing them on. When I go abroad and I see Barcelona, Bayern Munich, they might play a team a year younger in tournaments to see how they get on. Our best under-18s are playing under-21 and you want to push people forward."

Brady has been singing the same song for some time: "We've got one of the best youth systems here in England, if not Europe," he said in 2003. "And we've got a lot of talented young players, and quite a number of them who I believe will be Arsenal players in the future." A realistic prophecy or just a wish fulfillment? Unfortunately, the evidence points to the latter. As far back as three years earlier, Brady claimed: "In the next two years I hope to have the satisfaction of seeing [some of] the boys get into the first team. That's always the criterion, but at Arsenal there [are] double criteria – they have to be good enough to win trophies. They're not there to get into the first team and get sold on." This overenthusiastic forecast was corroborated by Arsène Wenger a couple of years later, having made a similar claim to a friend, who asked him whether anyone from the Academy "will be in the first team in a couple of years?" Wenger replied, "I tell you, there are half a dozen who really have a chance. Really promising players." Hopefully in 2014, no such rose-coloured spectacles were in evidence when reports suggested that the standard of young English players emerging from the Academy was giving cause for optimism. Chuba Akpom had graduated with honours, whilst the likes of Tafari Moore, Stefan O'Connor, Ainsley Maitland-Niles and Alex Iwobi were all highly regarded England youth internationals, and schoolboy Chris Willock had already trained with the first team. However, the usual caveat still applies and it remains to be seen how much of this youthful promise will actually materialise in the long term.

Brady's willingness to subscribe to the irrelevance of results may just have an element of post-rationalisation to it. Frequently, the under-18 side is made up of schoolboys, who supplement the remaining scholars who are unlikely to make the grade, and naturally results often suffer as a consequence. In 2013/14, the team failed to win a single under-18 Premier League game between September and January, and finished in ninth place in a division of 11. Conversely, in the cup competitions at youth level the selection policy has followed on from the increased importance Arsène Wenger now attaches to the FA Cup and the League Cup; in 2013/14 he selected strong line-ups in both competitions, thereby restricting the opportunities fringe candidates had to obtain a first-team appearance for their CV. First-team squad members such as Carl Jenkinson, Ryo Miyaichi and Gedion Zelalem have all featured in the under-21 Premier League Cup, whilst in the under-19 UEFA Youth League, the club ensured that Chuba Akpom was available to play under the terms of his loan deal with Coventry. So it was no surprise that Arsenal progressed to the latter stages of both competitions with the hope that, despite the inadequate league form at under-18 and under-21 level, the club might be on course to win their first youth trophy since 2010. However, in March 2014 both the under-19s and the under-21s lost their semi-finals to Barcelona in the UEFA Youth League and to Reading in the Premier League Cup respectively. And Chelsea made it an unwanted treble of semi-final exits when they defeated the under-18s in the FA Youth Cup a couple of weeks later.

An unvarnished assessment of the Academy can be seen from the club's self-congratulatory announcement of the renewal deals signed by five young British internationals (four English and one Welsh) – Wilshere, Gibbs, Ramsey, Oxlade-Chamberlain and Jenkinson – under the proud gaze of Arsène Wenger. Trumpeted as stars of today and tomorrow, Ramsey and Oxlade-Chamberlain had been pricey purchases as teenagers from Cardiff and Southampton respectively, whilst Jenkinson had been bought more modestly from Charlton. Theo Walcott also extended his stay the following month, and he, like Oxlade-Chamberlain, had been expensively acquired from Southampton at the age of 16.

So a nucleus of domestic players was now considered of benefit to the club after the penny had finally dropped that continental prospects would more often than not up sticks once their value soared, in tandem with the increased wages they could earn elsewhere. Analogies were made with the Manchester United class of '92 when Ryan Giggs, David Beckham, Paul Scholes, Nicky

Pre-season 2013.
Hands-on as always,
Arsène Wenger leads
training.

Mesut Ozil. His signing
represented a dramatic
change in Wenger's
transfer policy.

Aaron Ramsey (right) was voted the club's player of the season for 2013/14.

Mesut Ozil joined three other German first-team squad members at Arsenal, including the 'BFG', Per Mertesacker (below).

Arsène Wenger tried, but failed, to strengthen his striking options, leaving Olivier Giroud to shoulder a heavy load.

Mesut Ozil's first season at the club was inconsistent. Is the best yet to come?

Arsenal recorded their first triumphs at the new Wembley, winning in the semi-final and final of the FA Cup…

… leading to a day of celebration in the glorious Islington
sunshine after lifting their first trophy since 2005.

The story continues. Within a fortnight of the victory parade, the club announced that Arsène Wenger had signed a new contract to manage Arsenal for a further three seasons.

Butt and Gary and Phil Neville emerged in one fell swoop from the United youth set-up, the best academy system of its day. However, these teenagers had participated in two successive FA Youth Cup finals in the early 1990s before making the transition to the senior set-up, henceforth becoming integral elements of the club's first team. From Arsenal's 2009 version, only Jack Wilshere had made that leap. Back in 2000, Brady optimistically said: "The benchmark is what Alex Ferguson did at United. In striving to get his first team right, he made sure his youth policy was following on behind and we want to get ourselves into that position. I think we can."

It is a beguiling notion that Arsène Wenger would like his men to be seen in a similar light to the great Ajax sides of the early 1970s and mid-1990s, and the Barcelona team of 2011 in terms of enjoying a reputation for aesthetically pleasing winning football carried out by a healthy sprinkling of graduates from the youth system after a fruitful period of incubation as they developed and matured. At both clubs, the way the seniors play has been copied by the juniors at all levels, thereby facilitating a smooth transition through the ranks from the bottom to the top. The same strategy is applied at Hale End and London Colney, which begs the question as to why so few come all the way through the system and reach the requisite standard in north London.

Indications that Arsène Wenger may have given up on the Academy's produce could be read into the appointment of former West Ham stalwart and former West Ham and Tottenham youth coach, Pat Holland, as the manager of Arsenal's under-18s team in the summer of 2012, replacing Steve Bould, who took over the role of first-team assistant manager from the retiring Pat Rice. Strangely, in the light of his background, Holland was anything but a Wenger-style operator, with reports that his methods were old fashioned; his players were required to dress smartly before games and his reported touchline instructions like "cross it in" and "get tight" were out of keeping with the way the youngsters had been coached up to that point. He left after only seven matches, citing "personal reasons", although if the reality was that his way was at odds with the existing ethos, who exactly appointed him? And did the person ultimately responsible for the overall playing strategy even care? And maybe Holland, a man well versed in youth development, was on the right lines and the club incorrect in their approach? The possibility that there were issues still to be resolved was reinforced when, after the 2012/13 season, Miguel Rios, Ose Aibangee and Shaun O'Connor left the club and subsequently helped to transform the organisation and recruitment of Brentford's academy.

Liam Brady was a truly great footballer. At his peak, for Arsenal, Juventus and the Republic of Ireland, he was one of the most gifted, creative midfielders of his generation. Brady won two *Serie A* titles with Juventus and is fondly remembered to this day by the Turin *tifosi*, both for his supreme skill and his unexpected courage. Although aware that he was to be released and replaced by Michel Platini as the foreign star for the following season (1981/82), in his last game, when a win was required against Catanzaro to secure the title, a vital penalty kick was awarded. Most of his colleagues shirked the responsibility, but Brady stepped up and scored the goal in a 1-0 win. However, he did not cut the mustard as a manager, either at Celtic or at Brighton, perhaps in part due to a trait he possibly shared with other midfield maestros such as Platini, Hoddle and Gullit: to appreciate that more slack had to be cut and more patience needed with the obviously less talented players under his control, who should not be condemned by his own high standards; man-management skills that one would have deemed essential for a head of a youth academy.

Not a man to suffer fools gladly, Liam Brady is probably a paid-up member of one of the old school clans who felt that having played the game at a high level provided you with an inbuilt analytical advantage over any journalist or supporter. An excellent pundit for Ireland's RTE, along with his colleagues Eamonn Dunphy and John Giles, they put most English equivalents to shame with their insightful, no holds-barred observations. However, any negative comments from an outsider on his work as the head of the Arsenal Academy were brusquely dismissed out of hand and the perpetrator treated as if Brady believed life was too short not to carry grudges.

Prioritising Arsenal to the point of discarding objectivity was a rare case of ingrained loyalty that Brady shared with David Dein. Above all, the former vice-chairman loved the players, particularly the outstanding ones like Brady. He was influential in Brady's appointment as the youth boss, saying at the time that: "He [Brady] had the most important job at the club." The only conclusion that can be reached on Brady's tenure, putting to one side Dein's enthusiastic hyperbole, is that by his own criteria the Academy has manifestly failed to strike it rich. With the final judgement on Jack Wilshere as an outstanding international yet to be made, how condemning of the academy system is the fact that the only undeniably outstanding graduate, Ashley Cole, could not even be kept in-house; a world-class defender whose most rewarding time, to Arsenal's chagrin, was spent in a Chelsea shirt.

With hindsight, Cole's financial demands, which at the time earned him almost universal opprobrium from his erstwhile loyal following – 'Cashley Cole' was one of the more acceptable sobriquets he was given – do not appear unreasonable within the materialistic world of Premier League superstars, of whom he was undoubtedly one. For some long-term supporters like Martin Wengrow, his departure still rankles: "Ashley Cole was an Arsenal fan as a kid. He had Arsenal blood running through his veins. How disappointing that the club couldn't keep one of their own. I still get angry talking about it."

The days have gone when, as Brady put it in 2000: "The name of Arsenal was good enough for a boy to want to join, but things change when you could offer a boy a professional contract... whereas before I arrived they wouldn't be offered a contract until after they had proved themselves. The ones who were sought after would go elsewhere." This implies that 'elsewhere' the rewards were too attractive to turn down. Perhaps Arsenal took longer than their rivals to realise that, unless they were prepared to get their hands dirty, they would be left by the wayside. As recently as 2012, the residual distaste of how they now have to behave in order to acquire kids at all levels was probably shared by all the long-time servers at the club – a senior director dismissively categorised all agents as "parasites" – all the way down the line from Highbury House to Hale End. As Brady said: "You have to deal with agents, particularly if you are bringing someone in from another club, whether they are 14, 16 or 18. I've got agents ringing me up now telling me about a 14 year old at another club. We've got no option. We have to do it [contemplate signing under-10 year olds] if they go and join another London club, they can settle there. They have their mates. So there is real competition to get the best 7, 8, 9 year olds going on at the moment."

The emphasis at Hale End is on technique rather than tactics, with young boys judged by their skills and the priority in competition being possession, passing and creative ability rather than denial of the opposition. At junior level, this approach must be regarded as laudable, but whether it produces the finished article cut out for the rigours of top-flight adult football in England is debatable. It is interesting to note that a player such as Jack Wilshere, as well as being technically proficient, does not shirk the physical challenges. There is little indication that this aspect of his ability was encouraged in his early years at Arsenal, even though it has subsequently served the club well. Wilshere has admitted that going out on loan to Bolton taught him the importance of possessing a will-to-win approach, as exemplified by his then teammate Kevin Davies. On the other hand, though he did not make any significant impression at Norwich, once he returned home Kieran Gibbs progressed so well that he was soon capped by England.

However, loan players who have returned to the Emirates and subsequently captured a first-team squad place are few and far between. Certainly, the time spent by Wojciech Szczesny at Brentford and Wilshere at Bolton was entirely beneficial, but many others even fail to hold down a regular starting place in the line-up of their temporary lower division sides. But even that experience can be useful with the right attitude, as Chuba Akpom testified. He followed the well-trodden path to Brentford's Griffin Park, but only made a handful of appearances in a short stay. Nevertheless, as he told the Brentford fanzine, *Thorne in the Side*, he felt the move "benefited me a lot. I compare it to going to a good school, you learn good things, I learned what it was like to slot into a new team and it was a very good month. There were certainly things at Brentford that I can take back to Arsenal. I was really surprised at the organisation and attention to detail and professionalism. Everyone knows what they are doing. I would tell any young player that the experience is fantastic for their development; great staff and good training." On the other hand, though Akpom collected half a dozen first-team appearances, his stay at Coventry ended early and he returned to Arsenal with the words of the Coventry manager, Steven Pressley, ringing in his ears after a defeat at Brentford of all places: "I think we have a slight problem in respect of loan players and certain players coming to the end of their contracts," warned Pressley in the *Coventry Telegraph*. "At the end of the day, they return to their clubs or leave at the end of the season and it's not their concern [the club they have been on loan at] because it doesn't affect them moving forward. But for me and the fans, it's a huge concern and I have to make sure we've people here with the right attitude."

Perhaps Arsenal needed to be more meticulous when deciding how to use the loan system and could certainly have considered following Chelsea's example with Vitesse Arnhem in the Dutch league and Udinese's with Watford in the Championship; the senior club parks a large number of their employees at one specific well-run club on the basis that they would not be going just to make up the numbers. Chelsea had four of their youngsters with Vitesse over the course of the 2013/14 season, an arrangement facilitated by the relationship of Vitesse's new owner, Russian billionaire Aleksandr Tsjigirinski, with Roman Abramovich. However, subsequent accusations that Chelsea exerted undue pressure on team selection and went as far as reportedly attempting to hinder the Dutch club's quest for Champions League qualification (initiating an investigation by the Dutch FA) cast an odd light on how the loanees might get full value from their foreign sojourn. Both Watford and Udinese are owned by the Pozzo family, which has enabled the Championship club to loan or buy the pick of Udinese's players, such as the capped Italian striker Diego Fabbrini, one of seven imports, in a move presumably sanctioned by the owners on the basis that the financial rewards (specifically, a possible slice of Premier League pie) are so much greater than in Italy.

In order to provide regular action, albeit at lower levels, and maintain match fitness in lieu of just training and sitting on the bench, the loan system was espoused as the only way of acquainting the players with the physical demands of first-team football. But the powers that be had other plans: stipulating that a number of fixtures must be held in the club's main stadium, negotiating for a broadcast deal and, most importantly, introducing promotion and relegation, the Premier League believed that the modifications they intend to carry out to the under-21 structure in time for the 2014/15 season would obviate the need to send the boys away, improve the competitive nature of the contest and build invaluable fan support. However, the regulation that a maximum of only three over-age outfield players can be fielded in an under-21 team has reduced the likelihood of coming up against seasoned professionals on a regular basis, which was one of the advantages of the loan system and the old reserve league. Thus, the underlying problem of lacking the necessary preparation for the realities of first-team football, however favourable the opportunities for them to develop technically, will remain. The new format may be no substitute for going on loan and getting the experience of playing against mature, experienced professionals whose win bonus is an important part of their salary, and in front of crowds who may quickly turn on the loanee if they feel they are letting their club down.

With hindsight it is apparent that better use of the Academy might have saved Arsenal significant sums. The acquisitions of Walcott, Oxlade-Chamberlain, Ramsey and Jenkinson were estimated to have cost the club some £25 million. The reality is that, when a 16 year old is bought for a substantial sum by the club, he is immediately integrated into the first-team squad, giving the impression that the manager is generally not going to use anyone whose development he has not personally supervised. So the path of even the best Academy graduates tends to terminate with the reserves. They are then generally loaned out at some point with a view to their eventual sale; Wilshere and Gibbs are the rare exceptions who have returned to claim a first-team berth. The Hale End lads rarely get a look-in despite Brady's hopes for them in 2003: "You can't have a great football club without having a foundation from the youth," he said. "No matter who the manager is, that foundation must be really, really strong and I think that if you keep on doing the right things and keep on working hard, and I'm sure we will, then the investment the club have put into youth will pay very rich dividends in the years to come. I think there are hard times ahead for football and they are here already. I think that clubs are probably going to have to be more dependent on young players. And it will only be a good side if you're ready when that day comes with good young players. I'm confident we will be."

But the reality was that Arsène Wenger probably did not share Brady's vision. Talking about potential "Arsenal players in the future", Brady stated emphatically in 2003: "If they were at 80–90 per cent of Premiership clubs, they'd have had their chance by now, but that doesn't mean to say that the manager is mishandling them." Maybe not, but the sheer numbers of Academy developed players who have been sold on and played a minimal part in the club's first-team story since the arrival of a certain Monsieur Wenger, the former head of youth development at the then *Ligue 1* club Strasbourg, is astonishing, even allowing for the reality that statistically most will fall by the wayside. Those responsible for nurturing young talent at Arsenal can only feel a sense of disillusionment that so many who have been on the books as youths fail to come through the system for the playing, as opposed to the financial, benefit of the club.

In 2014 the 20 Premier League clubs between them had some 350 teenagers aged between 16 and 18 on their books, who have often been persuaded to compromise their education and social life in the mistaken belief that they will become professional footballers. This is far too many. And the dispiriting loss to the game is magnified between the ages of 18 to 21 when over 75 per cent leave with their dreams in tatters. (In the summer of 2013 Arsenal released over 20 players, the vast majority of whom were part of the reserve or youth teams whose contracts had expired and were not renewed.) The alarming statistics are reflected by the dire situation of the under-21s at Arsenal. The ever-changing format of the under-21 Development League, which is billed as the finishing school for the EPPP, will see the current league of 22 clubs transformed into two divisions with promotion and relegation from 2014/15. As a consequence of finishing in the bottom half of the 2013/14 league table, Arsenal will be playing in the second division.

Of course, what is intended at junior level could easily be applied at the summit to the betterment of the entire professional game. Premier League 2 should be formed. If the broadcast money was then split 80:20, the pervading fear of failure and the cost and stigma of relegation would be mitigated and the nepotistic parachute payments rendered largely unnecessary. Money would not be the omnipotent force it is. An innovatory coach, a good youth policy and judicious use of the transfer system would all have more opportunities to express themselves. The system would have more fluidity naturally built in. Clubs, players and coaches would move up and down the two divisions. A wider meritocracy would be established with the lower clubs having a greater chance of progressing through the divisions. Of course, the Football League could help themselves if there was a maximum of 20 clubs per division, and if at the bottom they were regional, as at long last there would be a pyramid structure rather than the four division ladder there is at the moment. There would be an overall rising of standards with many more English players coming through, even if no quota system was imposed.

A review by the FA and the Premier League in 2012 saw Arsenal warned – they were criticised for their management and leadership – that they were at risk of losing their category 1 academy status, and with it the attendant prestige and funding, to say nothing of the embarrassment. Worryingly, some of the brightest prospects had rejected the offer of a scholarship. One pertinent example was Jordan Brown, a striker who had scored regularly at under-18 level, but left in 2013 to join West Ham as he felt he would get more chances there as Arsenal possessed an abundance of young strikers who might have blocked his path.

Another concern for the authorities was the fact that the Academy was being filled from abroad or other London clubs, with very few pupils and students making the journey all the way from the under-9s to the under-21s. Indeed, the club gave scholarships to 17 youths in 2010, many of whom were the products of Hale End, but by 2014 all of them had left the club, with none of the English youngsters from that group having made a first-team appearance. Of the last 2013 scholarship intake, four were acquired from other clubs – Gedion Zelalem (Olney Rangers, USA), Renny Smith (Chelsea), Dan Crowley (Aston Villa) and Julio Pleguezuelo (Barcelona) – at the ages of 16/17, whilst Tafari Moore was signed from QPR at the age of 14.

For a club of Arsenal's stature and resources to be downgraded would have been a humiliating rebuke. With success stories so thin on the ground, in spite of winning the FA Youth Cup three times and the FA Premier Academy League five times during Wenger's tenure, legitimate concerns were raised over whether a top ranking was justified. The loss of funding could have been easily assimilated, but more wounding would have been the restricted freedom to sign lower league kids and the damage to Arsenal's reputation, contravening the manager's supposed predilection for giving youth a chance. Certainly, the facilities enjoyed by the youngsters are second to none, so the criticism was centred on the coaching methods and recruitment criteria.

A decision was made that a new direction was urgently required, and as a consequence Brady would vacate his post in May 2014 to extend his role as a club ambassador. (He was already an ambassador for the Arsenal Foundation, which supported a number of charitable causes.) In an appointment that augured well, Andries Jonker, whose considerable experience included that of a senior coach in the KNVB, the Dutch Football Association, as well as managing the national under-15 and under-21 sides, left his post as assistant manager at *Bundesliga* side Wolfsburg to take over Brady's job in July 2014. The fact that Jonker was the choice of Ivan Gazidis, who led the search for Brady's successor rather than Arsène Wenger, was perhaps an indication that the manager could expect more 'help' in future from the board. Hitherto, senior management appointments had invariably come from within and were initiated by Wenger. Not this time. Andries Jonker was a complete outsider. And the impression that Wenger would in future have less control over the Academy and youth teams was underlined when, in April 2014, two months before he officially started, a raft of Jonker-inspired changes, including the arrival of two fellow countrymen, Frans de Kat and Jan van Loon, overhauled the personnel set-up at under-16, under-18 and under-21 levels. Time will tell whether the new Dutch broom will sweep any of his charges into a long-overdue place in the first team.

Chapter 7

More of the Same, Please

At 1-0 down in Naples, and Dortmund apparently unable to get the better of Marseilles (down to ten men and pointless so far in the Champions League Group F), Arsenal were going through to the knockout stages as the group winners with their hosts going through in second place. But two late goals completely transformed the scenario; Napoli's 2-0 victory condemned Arsenal to the runners-up spot, whilst a late Kevin Grosskreutz goal earned Dortmund a 2-1 win and secured their qualification as group winners, eliminating Napoli in the process.

Arsenal fielded an experienced midfield against Napoli, but the absence of Wilshere, Ramsey and Walcott, all fit and available but not selected in the starting line-up, illustrated their limited Neapolitan ambitions, which was a shame when a draw would have guaranteed top spot and put them in a good position to progress as their last 16 opponents would be drawn from the qualified runners-up. Now it didn't take a pessimist to envisage Arsenal once again having to face one of the favourites and going out at the first knockout stage for the fourth year in succession. On the other hand, actually reaching the last 16 stage had been no foregone conclusion after a tough draw in the group stage.

This Arsenal team were no 'Invincibles', so the unbeaten run of four league games from late November to mid-December, which confirmed their place at the top of the table, had to end sooner rather than later, most likely at the home of one of their chief rivals – and first up was Manchester City. The setback in Naples proved to be a harbinger of possible bad times to come. Arsenal fielded an attacking line-up at the Etihad Stadium – Ramsey, Wilshere and Walcott all returned – but to no avail, unless scoring three goals away to City was an end in itself. Unfortunately, Arsenal were at the wrong end of a nine-goal thriller. Aided and abetted by some slovenly defending and poor officiating, City's attackers ran riot to devastating effect. Conceding six goals, though, cannot be defended (pun intended), however extenuating the circumstances. Wenger agreed: "Our strength until now has been our defensive discipline, but we lost that as the game went on. Whenever we got a goal back we conceded another soon afterwards, and always through bad mistakes. What hurts me more is that we had the opportunity to win and put City nine points behind us." The performance was certainly not the ideal preparation for the next key encounter, at home to Chelsea, which would be another testing examination of Arsenal's credibility as title contenders.

Unlike Wenger against City, Jose Mourinho sent his men out with the task of stopping their opponents from scoring. The negative tactics succeeded in sucking the life from the game and a no-score bore draw was the outcome. The shocking squally weather was some excuse for the insipid fare on offer from both sides, although it was unlikely that Chelsea's approach would have been any different on a fine spring day. Arsenal could regard the result as a point gained rather than two surrendered, provided they continued their winning ways against all and sundry below the top five. In effect, they had to try and take maximum points from their next seven games – West Ham away, Newcastle away, Cardiff home, Aston Villa away, Fulham home, Southampton away and Crystal Palace at home. A clean sweep of 21 points would set them up nicely for their next onerous assignment at Anfield in February.

In the first of these encounters, against West Ham on Boxing Day, Arsenal emerged triumphant thanks to a brace from the enigma that is Theo Walcott. Anonymous against Chelsea and guilty of a glaring miss before redeeming himself with his goals, Walcott came good against the Hammers, as did Podolski, who returned for the first time since his August injury.

With the holiday fixtures coming thick and fast, rotation was inevitable. For the rendezvous with Newcastle at St James' Park, Vermaelen, Ramsey, Arteta and Ozil were replaced by Koscielny, Wilshere, Flamini and Rosicky. Surprisingly, Giroud was not given any time off, but justified his retention by scoring the only goal with a deft header in a hard-fought encounter. Arsenal had now played all their Premier League opponents once, beaten most of them, and had accumulated the most points.

Another three days, another match and Arsenal entered the New Year as table toppers courtesy of a couple of late goals against

Cardiff at home. This time around there was no Giroud in the starting line-up; he was replaced by Podolski as centre-forward, who in turn gave way to Bendtner after 65 minutes. The 'Great Dane' put Arsenal on the scoresheet in the 89th minute, and this goal was followed by a second from Walcott in added time. It was a case of belated self-satisfaction after a difficult afternoon in dreadful weather against belligerent, aggressive opponents who were eventually worn down.

This third victory in a row once again demonstrated the team's resilience and ability to recover from the odd setback; the unexpected opening day loss against Villa, the expected reverse against Manchester United and the thrashing by City had not proved to be a precursor to a spell of dropped points, which had often been the consequence of an abrupt end to a successful sequence in the past. On the contrary, the Arsenal of 2013/14 seemed to be capable of putting each loss behind them and setting off again in a positive frame of mind. The last three fixtures – West Ham, Newcastle and Cardiff – demonstrated that the team was proficient in adapting to adverse circum-stances and emerging victorious, a pattern they would have to perpetuate unless they could overcome United, City, Chelsea, Liverpool and Tottenham when they next met them.

In the past, progress in the FA Cup had not been one of Arsène Wenger's priorities, with weakened line-ups being invariably selected and little account taken of the boost to morale that a successful run would undoubtedly bring. So it was a pleasant surprise that his men made light of what promised to be a difficult third-round tie with their north London neighbours. Despite ending with ten men – all sub-stitutes had been used and Walcott left the field on a stretcher with what was later diagnosed as a season (and World Cup) ending cruciate ligament injury – the two goals from Rosicky and Cazorla saw Tottenham defeated. The score was a fair reflection of an authoritative display that augured well when league duty was resumed just over a week later at Villa Park.

From the FA Cup line-up, Serge Gnabry retained his place, whilst Flamini, Ozil and Giroud all returned and Oxlade-Chamberlain made the substitute's bench for the first time since his injury against the same opponents in the first match of the season. Giroud marked his selection with a goal and ful-filled his allotted role, providing an outlet when the defence was under siege and ensuring that he kept the opposition defenders busy. However, with Walcott unavailable, the question of striking options assumed more importance, with too much dependence placed on Giroud maintaining fitness and form. Whenever the French international required treatment on the field of play, the concern amongst the supporters was palpable. When Arsenal came off second best to Villa on the opening day, legitimate questions were asked about the lack of transfer activity. Six months on, and with the imminent closure of the January transfer window, despite the satisfaction of a dif-ferent outcome – 2-1 to the visitors – the same questions were being asked, with once again the purchase of a proven striker seemingly an obvious requirement.

In the meantime, the winning run continued against Fulham at the Emirates. After a turgid first half, the home side created more space and put pressure on their opponents' defence, and Fulham eventually capitulated after two goals from Cazorla. Another three points were safely tucked away and, before the next Premier League fixture against Southampton, League One Coventry were the unlucky recipients of a fourth-round FA Cup draw which sent them to the Emirates.

The selection of Mertesacker and Koscielny at the back, Wilshere and Ozil in midfield and Bendtner as the striker to give Giroud a long-overdue rest for the Coventry game indicated that Wenger continued to take a conscientious course of action with regard to the FA Cup. Or was it that he didn't have much faith in his reserves, implying a lack of resources? As if to answer the question, Bendtner was withdrawn – for tactical reasons, not because of an injury – and then Giroud, soon after leaving the substitutes' bench, piled on the Danish international's embarrassment when he soon scored. On the other hand, perhaps Podolski's two goals prompted the manager to consider starting with him more frequently, if his post-match encomium was to be taken more seriously: "Podolski can score goals. When you have a good chance you want him to have it because he is a clinical finisher. He has an unbelievable short and quick backlift and he is very accurate in his finishing. He can score goals when he starts, when he comes on he is always dangerous."

Anyway, Arsenal ran out comfortable 4-0 victors. And with the same reservations about the team not being resilient enough to see off the two or three heavyweights in the quest to sustain a league challenge, if the cup draw enabled them to avoid the same opposition, it appeared that they might have a great chance to go all the way in a competition they last won nearly a decade ago. The significance of ending the trophy drought as a defining moment for an ambitious club cannot be overlooked; Manchester City won the FA Cup in 2011, their first trophy in more than a quarter of a century, and as much as the pleasure and joy City derived was an end in itself, more pertinent was the injection of confidence and self-belief to reach out and attain an even more notable bauble the following year, the Premier League title itself.

The progress that had been made through the third and fourth rounds of the FA Cup, together with five successive league wins in December and January, petered out at the end of the month in Southampton. Another foul midweek winter's night did not prevent the home team from demonstrating the quality of their passing and movement, and they could have wrapped up the match by half time. As it was, two quick second-half goals from Giroud and Cazorla gave Arsenal an undeserved 2-1 lead, which lasted only two minutes as a lapse of concentration by the defence gifted the home side an equaliser. After Flamini had earned himself a straight red card, adding to those of Koscielny and Arteta picked up earlier in the season and thereby dropping the club a few places down the Fair Play league, Gibbs replaced Cazorla to bolster the defence as the visitors settled for a draw. Even Arsène Wenger did not attempt to gloss over the deficiencies: "We played in second gear and Southampton in fourth. They played at a higher pace than us, decided to stop us from playing and did it very well." After another sub-standard away performance, at least this time they returned to London with a point.

On the plus side, the subsequent visit of Crystal Palace did not promise to threaten Arsenal's sequence of conceding just a single goal in their previous nine home league games. Better organised under Tony Pulis, Palace would hope to frustrate and then capitalise on any chance that Arsenal's carelessness and lethargy might offer them. Alex Oxlade-Chamberlain replaced the suspended Flamini in central midfield for his first start since August and duly rewarded the manager's faith with two well-taken goals.

Seven wins and one draw (22 points out of a possible 24) was an almost perfect return from the target that Arsenal had set themselves after being knocked off the summit on 23rd December following the draw with Chelsea. With the top spot regained, it was apparent that, with no reinforcements in January save the injury prone Kim Kallstrom, Arsène Wenger was banking on his current resources, in spite of the indisposition of Ramsey, Walcott and Wilshere, to see the season through to an ultimately successful conclusion. No thought seemed to have been given as to what he might do if he lost either Giroud up front or Mertesacker at the back for any length of time.

When Per Mertesacker joined Arsenal from Werder Bremen for £8 million in the aftermath of the 8-2 defeat to Manchester United in August 2011, he was exactly the kind of experienced defender – with 75 caps for Germany, including appearances in two World Cup semi-finals and a European Championship final – the club had been crying out for. Thomas Vermaelen had enjoyed two successful seasons, but a first-choice central defensive duo had not been established: Laurent Koscielny had initially struggled to adapt to the Premier League; Johan Djourou, despite showing promise, had proved inconsistent; and French international Sebastien Squillaci's form had not accompanied him from Spain to England. On the surface it looked like Arsène Wenger was collecting centre-backs in much the same way the former Arsenal manager, George Graham, had. The difference, though, was that all Graham's recruits understood the basic precepts of their job.

An exceptionally tall man at six feet six inches, Mertesacker compensated for his lack of pace with a peerless sense of anticipation, which enabled him to gain possession by stealth rather than having to commit to full-bloodied tackles; this was highlighted by the modest number of only nine bookings he had received in 221 *Bundesliga* appearances. He was, however, not the first Premier League debutant to be unnerved by the pace and physical demands of his new environment. A few weeks after his arrival, he commented: "I have to change my game a little bit. If you are new you want to help the team as an experienced player and a kind of leader, you want to settle in and adapt quickly. For me, it's hard work to have an important game every three or four days. That's very physical."

After taking time to acclimatise – his problem in tracking pacey forwards was picked up by the fans as well as opponents, although his many supporters were adamant that only an exceptional defender would have been selected so many times for his country – his commanding presence stabilised the defence, and after a shaky start the team consolidated their position in the top half of the table. Mertesacker was notably more vocal than Vermaelen, and due to his international pedigree and confident personality (in spite of only being 26) he commanded immediate respect in the Arsenal dressing room, which still featured a lot of younger teammates. "He is a good organiser," Wenger opined a few weeks after his arrival, explaining why he had brought Mertesacker to the club. "He understands the game, he is an intelligent player. Physically he's getting sharper in every game. We look less nervous at the back, and I think he contributes to that." Unfortunately, his first season was cut short when he suffered an ankle injury early in the New Year, and his enforced absence made the challenge for a Champions League spot more laborious than it probably would have been if he had been available.

By the time of his third season in north London, Mertesacker had become an automatic fixture in the first team, leaving Laurent Koscielny and Thomas Vermaelen to tussle over the right to become his partner. Mertesacker was able to reflect on how his game had developed: "I now have the nose and can smell the danger. I now know when my partner needs me to cover him. It's made me a better footballer. I anticipate and read the game even more because I maybe don't have the pace. I have to get by on my own qualities. I don't know if pace is needed to be a better player. When you compare me to Laurent [Koscielny, his habitual partner in 2013/14], he is more the mobile quick player. You need players like that and others like me with the organisation, the communication and anticipation." Moreover, the pair's complimentary skills and excellent understanding made the opponents' objective to isolate and exploit Mertesacker's lack of pace so much more difficult.

The German international and his French international partner also shared the invaluable habit of popping up with key goals, usually from set pieces. In the 2014 FA Cup semi-final against Wigan, Mertesacker netted the crucial equalising goal, whilst Koscielny repeated the exploit with the equaliser in the final against Hull City. Their partnership became the *de facto* first-choice centre-back pairing after the two played together in the unbeaten run of ten matches that secured fourth place in the 2012/13 Premier League, relegating Thomas Vermaelen to the sidelines. The duo continued the following season, with Vermaelen only used as a substitute or in domestic cup ties, at least until the FA Cup final when sentiment was put to one side and the club captain lifted the trophy after having played no part in the game.

Mertesacker was labelled the 'BFG' soon after his arrival in England, with reference to Roald Dahl's popular children's book *The Big Friendly Giant*, which was adapted to the language of the football ground in the chants the fans sang about him. He has become a cult favourite with the fans, who believe he 'gets' what Arsenal is about – "I love 'being Arsenal'," he said – and has been rewarded with a chant to the tune of the Cuban song *Guntanamera*, the chorus changed to the words "Big F***ing

German, we've got a Big F***ing German". The player himself was initially confused, recalling: "When the Arsenal fans first sang the BFG song, I was a bit unsure if it was a good sign or a bad sign." However, he has since embraced it and has a website selling t-shirts and other merchandise with the slogan for the benefit of his charitable foundation, which supports socially disadvantaged children around his hometown of Hannover.

Even though Mikel Arteta wore the armband on the pitch for most of the 2013/14 season, Mertesacker's authoritative demeanour, organisational skills and international reputation enabled him to take his colleagues to task when necessary. This was clearly seen when he read the riot act to Mesut Ozil at the conclusion of the 6-3 away defeat at Manchester City when his compatriot failed to acknowledge the travelling supporters, and when Santi Cazorla was also on the receiving end of a similar reprimand after carelessly squandering vital possession at Villa Park. Perhaps it is no coincidence that Mertesacker was also given the task of collecting player fines. (A notice pinned up in the dressing room at the training ground read "All fines to be paid in cash within 7 days of being posted" and included a list of the misdemeanours and their respective penalties – ranging from £1,000 for non-attendance of unused players at home matches without the permission of the manager to £100 for taking a newspaper into the dressing room.)[8]

---

[8] Other indiscretions in 2012/13 were punished as follows: late for training (less than 15 minutes) £250; late for training (more than 15 minutes) £500; late for treatment/massage (less than 15 minutes) £250; late for treatment/massage (more than 15 minutes) £500; late for travel £500; late for matchday meetings/meals £250; wrong kit on matchdays £100; inappropriate clothing outside of dressing room £100; newspapers, laptops and phones in medical room £100; non-production of urine sample for two consecutive weeks £200; phone calls in the building (texting allowed) £500; no participating in Commercial Activities (including Club Day) £500. All fines to be paid in cash to Per Mertesacker within seven days of being posted. If not paid within seven days – all fines will be doubled.

With such vast experience, and still at the peak of his powers, 29 years old being no age for a central defender, the manager's faith in Mertesacker was confirmed by the announcement of a two-year extension to his existing deal in March 2014, which would tie him to the club until 2017. He obviously felt that the club was in much better shape than when he arrived: "I think eight players have extended their contracts," he observed, "so the core is together and that has changed the belief, the togetherness, the confidence. We think we can achieve something."

An optimist reading between the lines might have formed the conclusion that Wenger felt that the squad which had rewarded him with the leadership of the Premier League going into February could keep him there, and there were no better available alternatives to the players he possessed. If so, he was in for a rude awakening when he went to Anfield for the first of a number of key encounters which would determine the ultimate destiny of him and his team.

Chapter 8

The Injury Mystery Tour

In April 2014 *PhysioRoom.com,* a popular website focusing on sports injuries and co-founded by Arsenal physiotherapist David Wales, identified that the Gunners had racked up 90 injuries during the course of the season to date compared to the fewer than 50 suffered by each of Chelsea, Liverpool and Everton. And it also emerged that this was not an atypical season. In a UEFA study published in 2011 which examined the injuries suffered by 50 top European teams, including Arsenal, the findings indicated that a player could expect to collect two injuries every season. Thus, in the mandatory first-team squad of 25 Arsenal should have expected to have to cope with around 50 injuries in 2013/14. Unfortunately, according to an analysis from *PhysioRoom*, Arsenal had averaged 66 injuries every season between 2002 and 2011, the worst being 2009/10 when they clocked up 86, an inauspicious record that they had already surpassed by April 2013/14. Perhaps it was no coincidence that when Gary Lewin left the Arsenal medical team to become the England head physiotherapist in August 2008, the injury rate increased by 28 per cent in the following season. Maybe, suggested a London Colney source, Lewin held more sway than his successors and their sports science colleagues. The insider felt that the advice of the club's medical team was sometimes too readily discounted by the manager.

The UEFA study also revealed that the average time a player could expect to be absent was 37 days in a season. But in recent years, Eduardo, Diaby, van Persie, Wilshere, Walcott, Vermaelen, Rosicky and Ramsey, all key first-team men, have missed many months and, in some cases, entire seasons. All the available data depressingly reveals that Arsenal have suffered both too many impact injuries (breaks, ligament damage) and too many soft tissue, muscle injuries (pulls, strains and sprains) than could be attributed to ill fortune alone. There was a deep-seated malaise somewhere in the house of Wenger.

The vital importance of accurate diagnosis and treatment at a top professional football club is explained by Ricard Pruna, the Barcelona club doctor: "We know today that if we go past a certain number of injuries we won't win the Champions League, it's impossible. That's a fact," he stated emphatically in 2014. "When we won the last two Champions Leagues [in 2009 and 2011] – I especially remember the one in Rome in 2009 – Barcelona had six muscle injuries [over the entire season]. That's a very low number. In other seasons when the club has maybe only won the Spanish cup but not the Champions League or the Spanish Liga, instead of those six muscle injuries we had maybe 40."

Unsurprisingly, there were almost as many theories as to why Arsenal should be affected so often as there were the injuries themselves, with one respected website, *Le Grove*, turning the subject into a *cause cèlébre* and prompting a media bandwagon. That Arsenal simply have more than their fair share of injury prone players can be dismissed out of hand. Bad luck is not a long-term affliction. There is no pattern to it. Misfortune cannot be anticipated; it is spasmodic and irregular.

The most popular theory advocated by the media is that Arsenal's injuries are to a large extent self-inflicted, namely that they are the consequence of the style of play favoured by the manager, his beloved obsession with possession, which puts the players at greater risk than if he employed a more direct approach. Former Arsenal midfielder Gilles Grimandi, who was appointed onto the scouting staff in 2005, put the argument as to why this might be the case simply and succinctly: "We have so many injuries because we keep hold of the ball more than other teams and this exposes the team to more knocks from opponents. It is also because we have a lot of small-sized players and the fact we take part in so many competitions increases the risk of injury [though, in fact, no more than any other top English clubs]." And he could have added that playing time, and therefore the chance of being sidelined, was extended by the many international call-ups, and that the situation was further aggravated when the intensive demands of the Premier League saw key players forced to return prematurely, thus making them susceptible to further trauma; Diaby's persistent muscle problems and Wilshere's third stress fracture, picked up on England duty in March 2014, which swiftly followed his tendon complications, just two of many examples. Certainly the high amount of possession, which is the cornerstone of Wenger's philosophy, invites more tackles being attempted by the opposition, and logic suggests that more tackles will lead to more injuries and also that small players are more vulnerable than large ones, although their size renders them less of a static target. Interestingly, an analysis by David Wall (from Opta Digital Sports Analysis) confirms that over the last five years Arsenal players have faced more tackles than those of any other Premier League team: 4,938, over 500 more than Chelsea in second place.

Dutch fitness coach Raymond Verheijen was on the coaching staff with the Netherlands, South Korea and Russia at three World Cups and three European Championships, probably as a result of being a *persona grata* of Guus Hiddink, and has worked in the Premier League with Chelsea and Manchester City. Whilst he goes along with the idea that there may be a link between Arsenal's style of play and the impact injury count, he dismisses the possession theory as the chief cause of Arsenal's woes. He told Radio 5 Live listeners in April 2014: "What we have left [aside from impact injuries] is a massive majority of soft tissue injuries, muscle injuries and that is something that has nothing to do with being in possession most of the time because if you are in possession you have to run less, you have to work less, [so in terms of muscle injuries] the majority of possession is actually an advantage."

In 2011 Arsenal opened a new medical centre at London Colney, specialising in long-term injury treatment, but maybe the priority should be prevention rather than cure. If Verheijen's view is accurate then a thorough examination of Arsenal's fitness, training and conditioning methods should result in a valid diagnosis. Perhaps Arsène Wenger's emphasis for training with the ball has been undertaken at the expense of conditioning work – he is not known to be an enthusiast for weight training as a regular slot on the timetable. Asked in 2004 whether the players used creatine (a controversial body-building supplement), Wenger replied "No." But when pressed, he admitted: "We had started one year, but that was because I was told that it was not [doping] and that it could help for recovery. But we then banned it completely, because some players put weight on. After I read more studies that it's like ten steaks in one – I hate it. I don't like weight. I think footballers need more coordination." However, Wenger is open-minded enough not to exclude weight training when he deems it absolutely necessary. Early in 2014 he subsequently revealed that: "In pre-season I saw [Yaya Sanogo] was under strength and not ready muscularly. We decided to take him completely out and try to build him up for four months – two months in France and two months with us. When he came back on January 1st, I saw he was a different [man]."

One area that Wenger should definitely be concerned about is the unacceptable number of injuries that have occurred in training; 11 members of the first-team squad during the 2013/14 season suffered in this way – Koscielny, Arteta, Wilshere, Flamini, Szczesny, Vermaelen, Cazorla, Walcott, Kallstrom, Gibbs, Diaby and Sagna – some on more than one occasion, begging the question of whether the phenomenon is peculiar to London Colney. According to Verheijen, Wenger's pre-season schedule is especially rigorous, and he went on to say that: "Teams cannot afford anymore to have 6–8 weeks off-season, so what you see now is that players only have 3–4 weeks off-season and they are relatively active with individual pro-grammes because if you lose too much fitness off-season it is very difficult to catch up pre-season."

The inference was that Arsenal were trying to compensate for the players' time off by their overly intensive pre-season schedule. He continued: "The most important thing is the way [Arsenal] do their pre-season. They have a very hard pre-season, almost like the Marines, and it is a well-known fact in conditioning that if you train your players too much too soon in pre-season that first of all you increase the injury rate and secondly you develop short-term fitness. In other words, fitness that only lasts for three or four months."

If Verheijen is correct then the traditional Arsenal training schedule could be the cause of the frequent falling off the pace in the New Year. Perhaps it was instructive that when Everton thrashed Arsenal 3-0 at Goodison Park in April 2014, the blue half of Merseyside were on top form after having won their previous six league games whilst Arsenal had only taken five points from theirs, a key factor being the absence of many midfielders. Wenger had his own explanation, simply attributing it to the fact that his team had played more games: "Everton went out very early in the League Cup and the FA Cup, and when you play in the FA Cup you play in [league] games which are postponed [to] midweek, plus the Champions League [as Arsenal have], so it is more difficult."

Everton manager Roberto Martinez disagreed: "I always believe every injury can be avoided," he told the *Daily Mail* in 2012. "I don't believe in soft tissue injuries. If you get a soft tissue injury in football, a mistake has been made." Naturally, Verheijen is in his corner: "For Roberto Martinez fitness is an integral part of football like tactics and technique, so they [Martinez's teams] are trained in football training by football coaches, but so is fitness. Roberto Martinez is responsible for the fitness training at Everton."

By not treating the subject with the seriousness it deserves, Verheijen suggests that Wenger has made a rod for his own back and that 2013/14 was even more of an injury prone season waiting to happen, with Aaron Ramsey's thigh problem a case in point. Injured on Boxing Day, Ramsey's time off was symptomatic of the rehabilitation process at Arsenal taking far longer than expected, the initial estimates for his return proving to be wildly optimistic, as indeed was the diagnosis for Podolski, who according to Wenger would be out for "eight to ten weeks" but didn't return to the first team for 16 weeks. Similarly, Oxlade-Chamberlain, Rosicky and Wilshere were all *hors de combat* for much longer than originally diagnosed, raising several questions about the expertise of the medical staff, whether their advice was ignored or, perhaps, that the hard pre-season had contributed to a propensity for unanticipated complications. Research by *PhysioRoom* has shown that Arsenal were without first-team players for a combined 1,716 days during the 2013/14 season, almost 300 more than Tottenham who had the next worst injury record. By contrast, Chelsea were without key players for just 556 days, while champions Manchester City and runners-up Liverpool endured an injury toll of 978 and 998 days lost respectively.

The extended absence of Aaron Ramsey hit the team particularly hard. The midfielder, who had been at Arsenal since being bought as a 17 year old from Cardiff City for £4.8 million in 2008, was absent for almost a year due to a horrific double fracture suffered at Stoke City in February 2010. As part of the rehabilitation process he went on loan to both Nottingham Forest and Cardiff City, before returning to play a handful of games as the 2010/11 season wound down. In the following two years Ramsey was invariably a regular selection, but until the final months of the 2012/13 season he had failed to convince observers that his injury had not impaired his potential. His finishing was awry and his passing lacked precision. For some in the Arsenal crowd he became an easy scapegoat for their ire. In December 2012, celebrity Gooner Piers Morgan asked on Twitter: "What DOES Wenger see in Ramsey?" after the announcement that the Welsh international had just signed a five-year contract.

Ramsey's chances of persuading the supporters that he was worthy of Wenger's confidence were not helped by the manager's preference to use him in a wide attacking role to which he struggled to adapt. However, there was a method in the perceived madness of apparently putting a square peg in a round hole, as Wenger explains: "It's sometimes a good idea to deploy a player who has a future in the middle of the park on the flank. He gets used to using the ball in smaller space, as the touchline effectively [restricts] the space that's available to him. When you move the same player to the middle he breathes more easily and can exploit the space better."

In the long term the ploy certainly looked to have paid off handsomely. Ramsey's contribution to the run in 2013/14 that took him and his teammates to the top of the Premier League and into the Champions League knockout phase was in a large part down to the goals he scored (eight in 18 Premier League appearances, with an even better strike rate in the Champions League with five in seven games) or the chances he created for his teammates. When he signed him in 2008 Wenger had compared Ramsey to "an offence-minded Roy Keane", but, though his work rate was remarkable, it was his improved finishing that took everyone by surprise; the 13 goals he scored before his untimely Boxing Day injury was more than the total he had scored in his previous five seasons at the club (albeit he lost a year through injury, of course).

Defensively Ramsey was an effective partner for Mikel Arteta or Mathieu Flamini and arguably showed greater awareness and discipline than Jack Wilshere, who is a year younger and was long thought among the football *cognoscenti* to be a much better prospect, until Wilshere suffered his own injury woes. The defensive aspect of Ramsey's repertoire came to the fore when he and Arteta were ever-present in the unbeaten sequence of ten matches at the conclusion of the 2012/13 season that propelled Arsenal to fourth place. Thus, he approached the new season (2013/14) with new-found confidence, saying he was, "100 per cent back mentally, 100 per cent into tackles, no hesitation, just clear again and free" and he attributed his subsequent dramatic step up to his renewed self-belief: "I just think you always have to believe in yourself. I always knew it was there."

Ramsey's penetrative runs, along with those of Theo Walcott, frequently took him past the main striker to the point of the attack and provided an outlet for the creative midfielders. Thus, the facility to inject pace into the attack was brusquely curtailed when, within a few days of each other, both suffered serious injuries; Ramsey on 26th December and Walcott during the third-round FA Cup victory against Tottenham little more than a week later.

Raymond Verheijen feels that the injury situation regarding the two players could have been handled differently or even perhaps prevented. In Ramsey's case he is critical of the time taken to return him to complete fitness. "If you look at his rehabilitation in the last few months," he told Radio 5 live listeners, "it has been a complete disaster. He pulled his muscle in late December and normally you are out for four or five weeks. After three setbacks, eventually his rehabilitation took more than three months."

Verheijen was even more damning regarding Walcott's cruciate ligament injury. The winger had already missed two months with an abdominal injury suffered in late August 2013 and had shown signs of good form when he returned, yet, according to Verheijen, his comeback could have been undertaken more carefully. In a *Daily Mirror* interview, Verheijen conceded that: "[Initially, Arsenal] brought him back really well. He played 25 minutes, then 25 minutes, then 45 minutes – so phase one of that rehab [was] building up match fitness. They gradually built up the game minutes and they did that really well." However, fixture congestion hampered his recuperation, as Verheijen pointed out: "Arsenal play two games a week, not one. This has nothing to do with match fitnesss, but you only have three days to recover not six days. You don't have the recovery time. They played Theo five times in 16 days, so instead of edging him in they played 90, 90, 90, 90, 90, so you accumulate fatigue, your nervous system becomes slower and this is one of the biggest reasons for anterior cruciate injuries. Such injuries often happen without the fault of an opponent. Often it happens with an innocent moment you've made a million times in your career. If he plays five times in 16 days, the nervous system becomes slower and his muscles around the knee are slower to contract, destabilising the knee. If the signal [to the brain] arrives a fraction of a second late then you are starting the movement with an unprotected knee, so you get injured. It's one of the main reasons why ACL [anterior cruciate ligament] injuries happen. The signal gets to the knee too slowly [when the player twists and turns] and the ligament ruptures or snaps."

And the Dutch fitness coach is also very critical of Arsenal's overall injury record. "Clearly something is going wrong. If you look at the law of the big numbers, something in the last ten years is going wrong. If it happens occasionally then this is a gut feeling. If it happens regularly over 10 to 12 years then coincidence is out of the question." Arsène Wenger himself seemed to be at a loss as to what was really amiss. In April 2014, he said: "Some of them [muscle injuries] are down to the medication that the players take that you don't even know about. Then you realise afterwards that they took this medication but that's not prudent ... If you lose your hair and you have taken something to make your hair grow it might not be good, especially for the rest of your body." After all these years in charge, Wenger comes up with the wacky suggestion that all these injury problems might have had something to do with hair supplements. Nothing to do with his coaching or training methods. Wenger continued: "I am concerned that this [high injury count] happens. We are analysing very deeply why it happened and to see if there is a link between all these injuries. For Walcott it is completely bad luck. Wilshere – I don't think it is linked with the other injuries, it is more linked with his history and the kick he got. But the rest maybe we have to find out why it happened." Asked by the press whether he would review his training and medical procedures, Wenger confirmed he would assess "everything," before saying: "It is very difficult to find any obvious reason why [we are having all these injuries]. Why? I don't know."

So is this promised investigation another instance of Arsène Wenger conceding, as in the cases of big money transfers and the youth policy, to some prompting from above for a change in strategy? His usual scathing response to hostile media questioning on his strategy is along the lines of: "I've been doing this job for 18 years, don't you think I know what I'm talking about?" But the fact that the more open attitude he showed during the 2013/14 season, and his admission of ignorance, was diametrically opposed to his usual stance indicated that he was very concerned with the state of affairs. Whatever the cause, the implication that "everything" by definition must incorporate his training and coaching philosophies and methods underlined that the investigation would be a watershed moment in the 18 years of his reign.

In July 2014 a positive first step appeared to be on the horizon. Previously reluctant to make changes to his backroom staff, Wenger looked as if he might break with tradition. Media reports suggested that Shad Forsythe, the fitness coach to the German national team – presumably endorsed by one of Wenger's former players, Jurgen Klinsmann, who hired him in 2004, together with the trio of Arsenal's German internationals – would be joining the long-serving Tony Colbert to enhance the fitness and conditioning resources at the club.

Chapter 9

Slipping and Sliding

At the beginning of February 2014, Arsène Wenger had many reasons to be pleased with his team's accomplishments. Thirty-five games done and dusted, and still in the hunt for three trophies. The league table saw them in first place with 55 points, two clear of both Chelsea and Manchester City. The next four matches – Liverpool and Manchester United in the league, Liverpool again in the FA Cup and Bayern Munich in the Champions League – would determine whether they became pretenders or would remain contenders. Of course, Wenger was no stranger to being in pole position on the front of the grid before being overtaken with the chequered flag in sight. This time, though, he radiated a confidence that had not been seen for a while, and the facts backed him up. Before the visit to Anfield, Arsenal had only conceded 21 goals in 24 Premier League outings, their best defensive record for six years. Though naturally delighted with the improvement – "We have more defensive stability, that is for sure. I think that is the main difference," he said – uppermost in Wenger's mind was the manner of the triumph against Liverpool at the Emirates three months before. "What happened on that day is that we dominated the game offensively," Wenger explained. "We have to not forget to attack. Our game is about that."

Perhaps he was lured into a false sense of euphoria by that 2-0 win and forgot that it had been the only occasion in the six months of the season that a Liverpool side which contained both Luis Suarez and Daniel Sturridge had failed to score. In no time at all, his delusions were shattered. In an amazing opening quarter, Liverpool consigned that November day in north London to an uncommon statistic. Liverpool manager Brendan Rodgers' game plan of starting matches at a furious pace to unnerve and unsettle their opponents surprisingly found Wenger's men completely unprepared for the assault. Four down after 13 minutes, Arsenal were simply discombobulated, overwhelmed by the pace and skill of Liverpool's attacking play, reminiscent of the way that Thierry Henry and co. had obliterated opponents in days gone by. Henry's Arsenal had reaped the benefits of the obligations first enforced by Tony Adams on Messrs Vieira and Petit, namely that defence began with midfield pressure. In 2014, it was the Liverpool pupils who taught the erstwhile masters a lesson they had apparently forgotten.

When Arsenal pushed up to try and give one of their central midfielders some support in possession, they were immediately engulfed by a plethora of red shirts who sealed off the passing options. Isolated, Arteta and Ozil were forced to retreat or attempt to dribble their way out of trouble, which Ozil tried and failed to do, leading directly to Liverpool's third goal. In fact, three of the goals came directly as a result of Arsenal losing possession in the midfield area (and the other two from the inherent inability to defend competently at set pieces).

After the break, Liverpool took their foot off the accelerator, but could still have ended up with more than the five they finished with. So much for all the bravado that when Mertesacker and Koscielny saw out the full 90 minutes together, Arsenal could expect to emerge unscathed. The Arsenal back four were simply brushed aside as the relinquishment of possession in midfield exposed them to the unrelenting pace and precision of their opponents, whose flexibility and movement enabled them to switch seamlessly from one system (4-2-3-1) to another (4-4-2 or 4-3-3) in the blink of an eye.

Almost as disconcerting as Arsenal's defensive fallibility was the fact that, despite being allowed the lion's share of possession in the second half, they were creatively inept. Mesut Ozil had another undistinguished day, his contribution so peripheral he might as well not have been on the pitch. So much for Wenger's pre-match strategy.

The lasting impression given by the Liverpool match was that a well-organised defence – and Liverpool's was not even tested on the day – could take care of Arsenal's attack, whilst their own would always be vulnerable to a swift, skilful counter-thrust, succinctly summed up by Wenger: "The performance overall was poor, on concentration and pace. We always looked vulnerable defensively." The vanquished were so inferior that the day could not just be dismissed as an unusually bad one at the office. Only one team had looked as if they had the stuff of champions and it wasn't the visitors. The obvious conclusion was that when Arsenal came face to face with top-notch teams, particularly in their own backyard, they would struggle to cope. Twenty-five games into the campaign and Wenger was forced to admit: "We have a lot of answers to find."

Ozil and Cazorla did not yet put one in mind of Bergkamp or Pires, and Olivier Giroud had not yet come anywhere near the level of Thierry Henry, Ian Wright, Nicolas Anelka or perhaps even Sylvan Wiltord. And of course there was no equivalent of Patrick Vieira, not only at Arsenal but in the Premier League, except in the persona of Manchester City's Yaya Toure (which brings to mind that Arsène Wenger, like Alex Ferguson before him, may have bought the wrong brother: Danny instead of Rod Wallace at Manchester United; and Kolo, despite his automatic choice as one of the 'Invincibles', was never the masterful force that Yaya has been at the City All Stars).

Less than a week after the Anfield embarrassment, Wenger was offered the opportunity for redemption and, just as important, the chance of an exceptional three points at the expense of Manchester United, who, after suffering a torrid season, had fallen down the list of dangerous foes. With tougher fixtures than the current champions in the offing, this home encounter was surely a safe bet for a title contender.

Perhaps the Anfield scars were still raw, at all events Arsenal were unduly conservative and unimaginative going forward against United, as if afraid of taking a sucker punch on the counter-attack. For their part, United were similarly limited in ambition, so what transpired was an insipid scoreless draw, a pale shadow of past high noon shindigs. The one point taken from the two contests with yesterday's nemesis was a poor return against fallible opponents.

The lack of creative spark in the Arsenal team highlighted how badly Aaron Ramsey's goals and penetrative runs from deep were missed. And the absence of pace – power had long since been mislaid – exacerbated by Walcott's indisposition, was largely responsible for Arsenal's jaded display, although no side with Ozil, Cazorla, Rosicky and Wilshere should have been bereft of inventive ideas. In retrospect, the occasion was a *carpe diem* moment and Arsenal did not seize theirs. Through negligible action on their part, having gleaned a meagre five points from four matches against Southampton, Crystal Palace, Liverpool and Manchester United, Arsenal only dropped to second place courtesy of Chelsea and Manchester City surprisingly only drawing at West Brom and Newcastle respectively. Even so, the lack of momentum at this crucial stage of the campaign was a concern, even if the table suggested the Gunners were still right in the mix.

Before the resumption of league hostilities, there was the small matter of Bayern Munich in the last 16 round of the Champions League, preceded by the fifth-round FA Cup tie against Liverpool. Fielding a weaker cup line-up in the light of the Champions League obligation three days later, a number of reserves – Lukasz Fabianski, Carl Jenkinson and Yaya Sanogo – were selected, with the young striker making his first Arsenal start.

Liverpool reprised their vigorous and forthright approach from a fortnight before and were close to opening their account on two occasions. On the balance of the chances created and referee Howard Webb's refusal to award them a second penalty, Liverpool should have emerged on top once again. As it was, the performance of Alex Oxlade-Chamberlain, feeling his way back after five months on sick leave, was the key factor; he scored himself and then set up Lukas Podolski for what turned out to be the decisive goal in the 2-1 win. Given Arsenal's good fortune, not least the fact that Wenger had got away with the gamble of giving a full debut to such an inexperienced youngster at centre-forward, the cliché about their name being on the cup seemed apposite.

Before the Liverpool game, the third home tie in succession, many supporters had been resigned to another season being 'over' prematurely, expecting that one cup exit would be followed in quick succession by another, with the resultant adverse affect on title aspirations. With the luck of the draw in the FA Cup as opposed to the Champions League, Arsenal received a shot in the arm and had a great chance to buck the trend and keep their season alive all the way to Wembley in April (for the semi-final), if not in May.

Unfortunately, the European trend established in the first knockout round over the previous two seasons, namely that of a first leg handicap that would prove to be insurmountable in the second, was set to continue. (At least against Barcelona in 2011 they were still alive after the first leg, but against AC Milan and Bayern Munich in 2012 and 2013 respectively they had left themselves with too much to do.) The decision not to start with Giroud for the first leg, almost certainly as a consequence of his illicit nocturnal shenanigans, merely highlighted the uninspired transfer strategy that now presented the manager with little choice but to select Yaya Sanogo for such a be-all and end-all match, thereby brutally exposing the lack of striking alternatives that was available to him.

Nevertheless, Wenger's team started well against Bayern and forced the holders into conceding an early penalty, earned by Mesut Ozil's skill and then unfortunately squandered by his lame attempt to convert it, with consequences far beyond the miss itself. "I think it affected Ozil," said Wenger. "He was still shaking his head five or ten minutes after that. It had a high impact on his performance. Confidence is your petrol in the team – it gives you the desire to play." Bayern's David Alaba was equally lackadaisical with his penalty attempt later in the half but, crucially, unlike their visitors Arsenal were reduced to ten men as a result of Szczesny's foul that led to their spot kick.

Most of the second half saw Arsenal restrict Bayern to a one-goal lead, but that was due as much to poor German finishing as to some spirited last-ditch defending. In the circumstances, the slender defeat would have been an acceptable result and hope would not have been extinguished for the return leg. However, late in the match an aimless free kick by Wilshere carelessly surrendered possession with Koscielny in the opposition penalty area seeking an equaliser. With the Arsenal defence in disarray as the centre-back attempted to regain his position, Philip Lahm, now operating in midfield, was able to cross for an unmarked Muller to earn his team a two-goal lead. At least Arsenal's performance had been a step up from the 2013 shambles at the Emirates. They had gone head to head against the holders until being reduced to ten men and, if Ozil had scored, the match might have taken a different direction and given Arsenal a far better chance in the return leg in Germany.

Six months earlier, Mesut Ozil had made his encouraging debut at the Stadium of Light, but for the home fixture with Sunderland he was left out. Despite the fans' initial pleasure at the manager breaking the habit of a lifetime and, for once, spending wantonly, Ozil now appeared an indulgence, just a luxury that could be afforded. But so could a few extra million pounds on Suarez, a true superstar who, unlike Ozil, had not only adapted to but thrived on the relentlessness of the Premier League. No hindsight was needed to bring home the point that there were sufficient alternatives in Ozil's position, but not nearly enough in Giroud's. So the chastised striker returned and obliged with a couple of goals in a routine 4-1 win; a job done with no anxiety, and keeping Arsenal one point behind the leaders Chelsea.

Next up was a visit to the Britannia Stadium on 1st March, which turned out to be a bleak reminder of past spring battles when Arsenal often faltered, Stoke having assumed the mantle of Bolton as the Gunners' most inhospitable hosts. True to form, the home side came out on top by showing more spirit and determination. "It is a big worry to lose a game like that," reflected Wenger. "We didn't produce the performance we wanted. To win a title when you are expected to perform, you have to perform. It's as simple as that. It was a massive setback."

The harsh reality was that Arsenal failed their more irksome chores. Certainly they emerged safe and sound from a multitude of easier ones, but unlike their rivals it looked like a case of so far and no further as the recent form guide (for the last six fixtures) for the top four teams illustrated: Chelsea 14 points, Liverpool 16, Manchester City 13 and Arsenal 8. Another case of déjà vu all over again, as expressed by the *Online Gooner* more in resignation than in anger: "One thing I noted about the game [against Stoke] yesterday is that watching it, I did not feel the desperation for Arsenal to win that I would have in seasons past. I was fairly philosophical about it. The players did not look particularly interested, so why should I? By the time of the Stoke goal I just felt a sense of resignation. I was prepared to hold off the feeling that a springtime collapse was inevitable, even if I had seen it more than once in recent campaigns when Arsenal have been well and truly in the mix as February turns to March, but after yesterday's game there seems to be a sense of the inevitable now."

With two cup games in the second week of March – an FA Cup quarter-final against Everton and the return leg with Bayern – rotation of the squad was inevitable. Thankfully, the usual suspects delivered the goods against Everton. After Sanogo once again failed to come up to scratch, he was replaced by Giroud who obliged with another couple of goals. Ozil and Arteta, with a coolly twice-taken spot kick, also weighed in to see Arsenal into the semi-finals with the prospect beckoning of a glorious end to the season. However, expectations were tempered the following day when, before Manchester City faced Wigan in the last quarter-final of the weekend, Arsenal knew that they would face the victors of that tie for their semi-final. Then, after drawing the short straw, they were unexpectedly invited into the box seats as the Championship side, away from home, repeated their astonishing feat of the previous season's final, once again overcoming arguably the most talented and certainly the most expensively assembled team in the country. Now there was a sudden surge of optimism amongst the fans that this season might after all end in glory, with the other two sides left in the competition being Hull City from the bottom half of the Premier League and League One Sheffield United.

A respectable result in Munich would administer further balm to the healing process, even if qualification to the next round was realistically beyond them. Once again they started too slowly. Schweinsteiger was afforded too much space in the penalty area and opened the scoring. However, Arsenal, aided by a large slice of good fortune when the referee ignored Podolski's blatant push on Lahm that gave him the space and time for his equaliser, were able to leave the competition with a creditable 1-1 draw. Looking back, the harsh fact was that they had failed to heed last year's German lesson. There was simply too much ground to make up after the first leg; sloppy moments and mistakes once more proved fatal.

Even so, Arsenal returned from Munich far from disgraced and they could recall that their 2013 victory in Germany, albeit academic, provided the impetus for an unbeaten sequence which they now had to replicate to keep their fading title hopes alive. In order to do so, though, they had to move up a gear, having so far failed to emerge with anything other than scant reward in the tussles with their main rivals. Tottenham, Chelsea, Manchester City and Everton now lay in wait between 16th March and 6th April, and despite the pitfalls Arsenal could have avoided, they had established a decent position for themselves. Still second in the table, now they had the opportunity to deliver and prove the naysayers in the stands and media wrong.

The first obstacle was Spurs at White Hart Lane, and Arsenal approached the game with the unexpected fillip of Chelsea's surprise capitulation at Villa Park the day before. In an explosive start, Rosicky blasted the ball into the net in the second minute and, moments later, Oxlade-Chamberlain should have made it 2-0 when put clean through on goal, but the kind of audacious chip he attempted was clearly not yet part of his repertoire. The early goal shaped the game. Tottenham made a wholehearted effort to restore equilibrium, enjoyed the majority of possession and territory, but it was to no avail as Arsenal resorted to absorbing the pressure whilst waiting for the chance to mount a counter-attack. Substitutions clearly indicated Wenger's defensive intentions and Tottenham eventually ran out of steam, unable to breach a defence excellently marshalled by Mertesacker and Koscielny.

With the first hurdle safely cleared, Arsenal had to rest, recover and tackle the next more onerous match against

Chelsea at Stamford Bridge. Although Chelsea were seven points clear at the top, Jose Mourinho suggested that the three games that Manchester City had in hand over them rendered the table "false." In response, Wenger's observation was that a failure to acknowledge that Chelsea were still in the title race was done so because they "feared to fail." His comment was a red rag to a bull and elicited a withering riposte from the Chelsea manager. "He [Wenger] is a specialist in failure, I am not. So supposing Wenger's right and I am afraid of failure, it is because I don't fail many times. I'm not used to failing, but the reality is he is a specialist because eight years without a piece of silverware, that's failure. If I did that in Chelsea I would leave London and not come back."

The scathing criticism raised the pre-match temperature to boiling point. Billed as the 'Special One' against the 'Specialist in Failure', the visit to west London was probably the last place the Arsenal manager would have chosen to celebrate his 1,000th match in charge of his club. After a week of gushing tributes from 'the football family', it was left to Mourinho to strike a sombre note of discord: "It's not possible to have 1,000 matches unless the club is also a fantastic club in the way they support the manager," Mourinho commented, "especially in the bad moments, especially when the bad moments were quite a lot. The tribute is to say that I believe that any one of us [managers] would love to have the same privilege with our clubs."

Any confidence Arsenal possessed before the start was blown away after just 17 minutes. Three nil down and forced to face the next 73 minutes with only ten men after referee Andre Mariner had wrongly dismissed Kieran Gibbs instead of Alex Oxlade-Chamberlain for handball on the goal line. Yet, the crass error should not obscure the fact that Chelsea had already taken control, and such was the poverty of their opponent's play that even if Arsenal had been allowed an extra man then only a fantasist could have envisaged any other result than a resounding defeat. A flashback. Just like the mortifying spectacles against Manchester City and Liverpool, the goals rained in after possession was carelessly relinquished by the Arsenal midfielders, thereby repeatedly exposing the defence to the pace and precision of the Chelsea attack.

The eventual 6-0 drubbing was Wenger's heaviest defeat as the Arsenal manager (ironic considering the landmark) and Mourinho's biggest victory at Stamford Bridge. Several issues were once again brought to the fore: Wenger's strategy and tactics in the biggest games, the selection and preparation of his men, the lack of spirit and motivation they showed, and his unwillingness to adapt to the specific threats that he knew he had to contend with. Shaken and care-worn he promised a thorough investigation into the day's events. "I take full responsibility," he said. "It is my fault that we failed completely because we did not turn up. It became a long, dramatic, dreadful afternoon. This is puzzling because we were shocked and knocked down. Basically without feeling you had a chance. The team is healthy and willing – we have to think deeply because it is not the first time."

Whether Wenger's *mea culpa* would be the first step on the road to recovery was in all probability irrelevant in terms of maintaining a title challenge in 2014. Teams that concede 17 goals in three matches against their chief rivals, compounded by a loss of consistency against the 'lesser teams' (the last five away results had been Southampton 2-2, Liverpool 1-5, Stoke 0-1, Spurs 1-0 and Chelsea 0-6) do not win titles. A total of 128 days in the number one spot (as it turned out, weeks longer than any of their rivals) counted for nothing, and the best that could realistically be envisaged was that, if Arsenal immediately re-established the previous winning ways against the less challenging opponents, enough of whom were due to be faced in six of the last eight matches, Champions League qualification might once again be attained.

Chapter 10

A Question of Support

"Who is Arsène Wenger accountable to?" Ivan Gazidis was asked in June 2011 at a Q&A event staged by the Arsenal Supporters' Trust (AST). "Arsène is ultimately accountable to the fans – they ultimately make judgement" was the CEO's response.

Taken at his word, the message was clear: the manager lived and died on the acceptance, if not the approval, of the supporters. Arsène Wenger had instilled incredible loyalty in a large section of the fanbase, so in spite of some spectacularly bad days, the groundswell of opinion demanding his removal had never reached fever pitch. Gazidis was therefore on fairly safe ground to suggest that it was the fans rather than the directors who controlled the manager's destiny.

Yet, in reality, how much sway did the supporters really have? The rare occasions when the wrath of the supporters had poured down on the manager's head could be counted on the fingers of one hand. Away to Fulham in the final match of the 2010/11 season, a large number of the travelling fans chanted, "Spend some f***ing money!" in frustration with the way the season had collapsed. In January 2012, flabbergasted that Alex Oxlade-Chamberlain was withdrawn after making a positive contribution against Manchester United, chants of "You don't know what you're doing!" rang round the Emirates. And the August 2013 opening day home defeat to Aston Villa witnessed a repeat of the Craven Cottage chanting. A more measured note of disapproval came from the AST in April 2011. The message – "There is considerable disappointment amongst all Arsenal fans at recent results in the cup competitions and the long period Arsenal has gone without winning a trophy" – was described by the chairman, Peter Hill-Wood, as "stupid comments from silly people. They are supposed to be supporters," he added, "but, in fact, they do quite a lot of damage." This was perhaps a more accurate reflection than the assertion by Gazidis of how seriously the board viewed criticism of the manager. The impression given by Hill-Wood was that the supporters were regarded as a nuisance, and certainly were not in a position to hold the manager to account.

Hill-Wood's statement, which caused outrage amongst the supporters' groups, was a step backwards in the relationship between the club and its fans, which in the preceding years had generally been closer than it is at many Premier League clubs. The Arsenal Independent Supporters' Association (AISA) was formed in 2000 to help the club to obtain planning permission for the new stadium, and the AST, which came into being three years later, worked closely with the club when Stan Kroenke took over. The arrival of Ivan Gazidis and Tom Fox, bringing with them their American sports marketing expertise to develop revenue streams, particularly in the commercial sector, necessitated a crash course in understanding English football culture and Arsenal football club. And what better way to learn than to enter into dialogue with supporters, particularly those from professional backgrounds. As such, Arsenal embraced the AST, who helped them to understand the brand and potential commercial opportunities, and became an integral part of the market research for the club.

Despite this initially comfortable relationship with the new executive, the AST has proven to be an independent body of substance due, in no small part, to the professional expertise – in finance, law, marketing and the media – of their key directors. Formed with the objective of widening the ownership of Arsenal and thereby increasing the effect supporters could have on club policy, the Trust courted small and large shareholders alike, and at one point their membership accounted for a 3 per cent block of the club's shares. They also introduced a scheme, 'Fanshare', whereby supporters could buy into the equity of the club for a more modest contribution than the price of a full share. (A single share at the time of the launch in August 2010 was more than £10,000.)

Developed in association with the club, the scheme allowed supporters to invest as little as £10 a month or make a one-off payment of £100 to own part of an Arsenal share. It was an innovative idea and was widely welcomed, even earning plaudits from UEFA. General Secretary Gianni Infantino remarked: "The growing influence of supporters' organisations in Great Britain, in this particular case via the Fanshare scheme at Arsenal FC, is good news for European football and strengthens the concept of Financial Fair Play. At a time when the global economic crisis and the lack of financial discipline threatens the very survival of many football clubs, supporter involvement offers a credible and sustainable alternative and we at UEFA welcome any such moves."

The then Sports Minister, Hugh Robertson, also commented: "Arsenal's proposal is an enlightened and forward looking way of doing this [greater supporter involvement] and makes it affordable for their fans to own a part of their club."

However, the continued success of Fanshare was dependent on there being shares available to buy. And the circumstances radically changed when Stan Kroenke, after acquiring the shares of Danny Fiszman (shortly before his death in 2011), Lady Nina Bracewell-Smith and the other directors, became the majority shareholder and was thereby forced to make a compulsory purchase offer to all remaining shareholders. But Kroenke was unable to force the club to go private, even if he had so wished, because he would not have been able to obtain the number of shares required (90 per cent), as Alisher Usmanov would not sell his holding, which by this time had grown from the 14.5 per cent (his initial acquisition of David Dein's shares) to over 25 per cent. Rather than sell, Usmanov's intention was to increase his stake to 30 per cent and he offered £14,000 a share (nearly £2,500 more than Kroenke was willing to pay) to any shareholders who wanted to cash in, and many regarded it as an offer they could not refuse.

With Kroenke unwilling to either donate, free up long-dormant shares or issue new ones, while Usmanov was increasing his holding, Fanshare's growth opportunities were severely curtailed. On the plus side, with Alisher Usmanov immovable the club retained its plc status; its statutory AGM was a regular event and their audited reports were readily available. This meant that the Trust's financial people, as well as bloggers such as the *Swiss Ramble*, were able freely to cast an expert eye over the entire ramifications of Arsenal's financial affairs, and highlight delicate situations concerning the wages, transfer budget and commercial revenues. Consequently, when large amounts of cash sat unused in the bank whilst there was a perceived lack of quality in the playing squad, increasingly relevant questions could be asked about the club's genuine ambitions. These were nakedly exposed by Arsène Wenger's poorly received observation that qualifying for the Champions League was like a trophy in itself. In his speech at the 2012 AGM, he told the audience: "For me, there are five trophies – the first is to win the Premier League, the second is to win the Champions League, the third is to qualify for the Champions League, the fourth is to win the FA Cup and the fifth is to win the League Cup. I say that because if you want to attract the best players, they do not ask, 'Did you win the League Cup?' they ask you, 'Do you play in the Champions League?'"

As the dust settled on the Kroenke takeover, the club and the supporters' groups have drifted further and further apart. Tim Payton, the Trust's chief spokesperson, recalled in 2014: "Before the change in the ownership structure when Stan Kroenke took over the club, the AST had good relationships with, and were frequently in touch with, the larger shareholders in Arsenal who sat on the board. This link between supporters and the owners was important and helped to create the feeling of custodianship and being a part of the club." Unfortunately, the Trust feels that the commitment in the offer document that Stan Kroenke made at the time of his takeover to "meet with supporters and fan groups" has not been adequately fulfilled. Since then, Kroenke has only encountered the Trust during his regular attendance at the AGM and, whilst he has addressed his fellow shareholders, he has never taken any direct questions. The most disappointing aspect of the situation is that the Trust had undertaken a key role in building bridges between Kroenke and the Arsenal board in the days when the directors were uncertain about the American's motives, but the relationship has waned since Kroenke came to power. Significantly, when the club's official website (*www.arsenal.com*) was re-designed in February 2013, the links to supporters' groups no longer listed the AST, and their promotion of the Fanshare scheme was put to one side once Kroenke took over. However, the Trust, due to their excellent links with the mainstream media and their extensive use of social media, remains a vital and influential voice. Payton, whose day job is corporate communications and public affairs advice, specialising in sport, has over 40,000 followers on Twitter. He claims that: "The pressure [exerted by the Trust in the debate] on ticket prices has helped to limit even bigger increases that Kroenke Sports Enterprises would like to introduce."

Despite some reservations regarding the way the club is run, such as the power that Arsène Wenger wields, the Trust has stopped short of calling for the manager's head. This reluctance to upset the apple cart is shared with the three other significant organisations that exist to represent supporters. The oldest of them, AISA, pre-dates the Trust and actually provided £1,000 to help to get it off the ground. Funded by membership subscriptions which number more than 1,000, AISA states its main area of activity as: "Making representations to Arsenal and to other organisations that can affect the enjoyment and the matchday experience of Arsenal fans, such as the police, the local council and the national football authorities." AISA also fundraises for Arsenal charities, such as former player and coach Bob Wilson's Willow Foundation, and runs a history project, which has encouraged the club to reflect the epoch events of the past. But perhaps its most important role is to be a spokesperson and a conduit on behalf of fans for problems or injustices that have arisen, most often related to ticketing. For example, AISA highlighted the raw deal that pensioners received (reduced price seat tickets were only available to OAPs in the family enclosure) and produced a supporters' ticketing charter with various proposals and changes it wanted the club to consider.

On the basis that more lower priced tickets would be made available to Arsenal supporters, AISA backed the club's policy of moving to three match ticket price bands. (From August 2012, the 19 home Premier League matches were split into five Grade A, nine Grade B and five Grade C, as opposed to the previous system of five Grade A and 14 Grade B). The new format reflected the attractiveness of opponents with a greater disparity in pricing, contrasting with the previously less flexible format. Although Grade A admission prices have shot up, AISA felt that if the 'cherry pickers' had to be penalised, it was a sacrifice worth making as the far cheaper Grade C prices would permit adults to watch the team for as little as £25 (the cheapest ticket under the old system had been £33) when the opposition were the likes of Swansea and Hull. However, AISA's observation in January 2013 – "Arsenal supporters sympathise with our counterparts at Manchester City, who are clearly embarrassed at their failure to sell a third of their tickets for Sunday's January 2013 match at the Emirates Stadium" – missed the point that it was Arsenal who should be embarrassed about charging the travelling fans £62 for what were nowhere near the best seats in the stadium. To their credit, AISA have stepped up their campaign for the price of away tickets to be lowered and capped, and for the club to recognise the loyalty of their thousands of fans who travel to away grounds.

AISA's ability to get their message out is hindered by their relative inactivity on social media in spite of the existence of a Twitter account, which is primarily used to address the misconceptions of tweeters who believe the organisation to be too eager to cosy up to the club's decision-makers. AISA would refute the charge, citing as an example the protestations it made to the club regarding the lack of consultation with supporters when the redesigned logo was launched in 2002. AISA are certainly less vocal than other groups, believing that, as a collective with a broad range of issues to represent, they are best served by engaging in an ongoing dialogue with the club rather than concentrating on sound bites on Twitter or Facebook. Their approach suits them, but many fans seek a more public response. As one former committee member comments: "AISA did a decent job [in the first few years of its existence] dealing with the police and council and putting across the fans' perspective in areas where they [the club] didn't fully understand the extent of the fans' problems. But since then they appear to have been rather lightweight and have clearly backed away from any major initiatives from fans that are even mildly controversial."

Believing more direct action was needed, in 2011 (the summer that saw Cesc Fabregas and Samir Nasri sold) a new organisation called the Black Scarf Movement (BSM) came to prominence. "It was felt that there wasn't an existing supporters' group that shared the concerns of many fans," explained one of their leaders, Kelvin Meadows. "AST is for Fanshare, REDaction [another significant supporters' organisation] is about generating atmosphere within the ground and AISA... well many were asking what do they actually do? They had [little] presence on social media and were deemed by some as a group of well-intentioned fans that toed the club's line on every matter. We felt the club needed to be made aware that there are a growing number of fans who are disenfranchised. Simply put, they love the club but feel the club no longer wants them."

BSM's methods were direct and very public. They organised protest marches on matchdays and leafleted shareholders attending the AGM. Their disgruntlement was with the way Arsenal was being run and, specifically, that the club was making huge profits but still charging high ticket prices.

Seen very much as the outsiders in terms of the supporters' groups, the BSM have no representative on the Fans' Forum. However, as Kelvin Meadows opined, it is not a matter of regret: "The Fans' Forum is a complete waste of time and is purely a PC tick box exercise." The forum is a formal meeting whereby elected representatives of different groups, for example 16–21-year-old members, family enclosure users and away scheme members, meet with club officials on a quarterly basis, usually in the Highbury House boardroom, before a nominated home match. Issues are raised in advance and, although an element of discussion occurs, it is for the most part an opportunity for the club to give official responses. Minutes of the meetings are posted on the club website, though with no great urgency, with delays of weeks not being uncommon.

Raymond Herlihy, a founder member of REDaction who represented the group on the forum from 2009–11, expresses the view that the body "is mainly lip service to say 'we consult with fans three or four times every season,'" although he believes its negligible effect is not solely the club's fault. "The people who make up the forum must take some responsibility for this as most do not have the right reasons for being there, or do not have the right personality for being part of it. I have seen some forum members contribute exactly zero for their two seasons [the standard term before having to present themselves for re-election]." Steve Cooper, who represents the AST, concurs: "The forum is a well-meaning attempt by the club to engage with supporter groups representing as diverse backgrounds as possible. Unfortunately, it is let down by having so many groups involved ultimately having their own agendas that help their own needs rather than the supporters as a whole."

REDaction is an informal collective of supporters who have been around since the Highbury days and whose aim is to improve the atmosphere at Arsenal matches. In many parts of the Emirates enthusiastic, vocal fans are frowned upon by their more inhibited neighbours, but not in the 'REDsection' seats in the north-west corner of the lower tier. As a result of an initiative devised between REDaction and the club, season ticket seats in this area are allocated to like-minded supporters who wish to gather to stridently back the team, although the group's plans for displays (often involving giant flags or banners) have sometimes been thwarted by the Stadium Management's health and safety concerns. Raymond Herlihy elaborated: "We still have regular battles with Stadium Management over what can and cannot be done within the stadium, and even the smallest of events need to be planned months and months in advance. However, this is still progress from how difficult it used to be five or six years ago. Arsenal are constantly worried about upsetting the vocal [in terms of complaining, if not singing] minority, so supporters must acknowledge the part they have to play in this – for every complaint about a flag, banner or supporters event, there is [an adverse] knock-on effect."

Gradually REDaction have been able to pull more strings, culminating in an impressive, stadium-wide red and white card display before the home leg of the Champions League tie in February 2014 against Bayern Munich. Every supporter, with the obvious exception of those in the away section, was given a red or white card to hold up as the teams came out, creating a mosaic featuring the word 'Arsenal' and the image of a cannon.

An attempt to establish a formal alliance between the four groups – AST, AISA, BSM and REDaction – produced a letter from all four requesting Stan Kroenke meet with them when he was in the UK for the October 2013 AGM. It received no response. A subsequent proposal that the four organisations combine to fight together on ticketing policies failed to get off the ground. Nevertheless, both AISA and AST lobbied independently and successfully for improvements to the club's online ticket exchange system, whereby, for a token fee, season ticket holders can sell their seats for individual matches. A proposal from the AST that the club provide cheaper tickets for youngsters led to the creation of the 'Young Guns' section behind the Clock End goal, where 12–16 year olds can buy tickets for Category B and C weekend matches for £10; a welcomed concession with further price reductions for teenagers and Friends and Family Days, as suggested by AISA, perhaps on the way.

To give credit to the club, there is no compulsion on the directors or staff to interact with supporters on any other occasion than the AGM. Kelvin Meadows admitted: "Arsenal, more than any other club, engage with their fans. However, it's a common belief they only talk to those that agree with what the board does." Yet, although this may be the perception, it is not borne out by the facts. The CEO can get plenty of flak at the Christmas drinks party the directors put on for the supporters' groups and at the annual end of season Q&A event he speaks at (although pointedly, the BSM are not on the guest list).

However, the person most people want to hear from is the most elusive of all. Although there had been Q&A sessions for the shareholders with the manager from 2008, these were quietly dropped after a couple of years as a result of the rough ride he received and because, as David Dein has said, "Arsène does not like confrontation."

An event that Wenger attends with a degree of equanimity is an annual end of season drinks for Diamond Club members. The atmosphere at these occasions is more convivial, perhaps because the manager feels more at ease in the company of the high earners (a season ticket cost £25,000 in 2012/13) than he does with the run-of-the-mill shareholders with their awkward questions seeking clarification on his methods.

None of the organised supporters' groups have this kind of access and, in that sense, have no specific reason to hold back in terms of direct criticism. For REDaction and AISA, their fundamental ethos is the relationship between the club and its supporters. REDaction even organised a show of support for Wenger back in May 2009 when there were fears he might join Real Madrid after a particularly fractious Q&A event with shareholders. At the time, REDaction's Mark Brindle said: "Arsène has worked miracles and people must not be so short term in their thinking. He is the man for this club and, if people drive him out, they would regret it." Before a home game around 100 fans marched from REDaction's pre-match drinking venue, The Rocket on the Holloway Road, to the roundabout on the west side of the stadium to sing songs of support for the manager. T-shirts with the message 'I love AW' were also distributed. The BSM might be no friend of the board, but steer clear of the issue of the manager for the simple reason that they do not wish to divide support for their underlying message that supporters are being driven out by the cost of admission. The AST questions the organisation of the club in terms of its structure (advocating in April 2013 a football advisory sub-committee to report to the main board, that takes more of a strategic view on departments such as youth development, player scouting and football coaching) and as such have been more likely to admonish the manager than any other group.

Another outlet for supporters, and a more immediate one, is found in the wide variety of online blogs about the club. Whether they have friends in high places is debatable, but they certainly play a part in shaping opinion and have tended to polarise the fanbase. The most widely read blog is *Arseblog*, an irreverent daily digest of news and opinion with links to stories in the media and on other websites. Established in 2002 by Andrew Mangan, *Arseblog* has gone from strength to strength. Probably the main factor in its continued popularity is its measured support for the club, even when being critical. Mangan is very cautious about writing anything that could be perceived as a knee-jerk reaction and plays down his own importance and that of his regular columnists in the ability to shape views. He says: "I've never felt that I'm someone who influences others. I've never assumed that I can speak on behalf of anyone but myself, and I don't see myself as any kind of figurehead. I accept that people enjoy the writing that I do and the other content we produce in terms of podcasts, columns, news, reports etc., but I think people are more than capable of making their own minds up about things." He may not wish to acknowledge his influence but, given his readership, it is undoubted and widespread.

More critical of the club is *Arsenal News Review* fronted by Myles Palmer, whose eclectic musings, not only on Arsenal but football in general and the music business, have generated a huge following over the years. Another reproachful voice is *Le Grove*, started by brothers Peter and Geoff Wood in 2007. Now mainly written by the former, under the pseudonym Pedro, Wood writes a provocative daily offering presenting an informed view of club matters that tends to chime with a growing number of disaffected fans. On the other hand, Wood's day job qualifies him to compliment the club when he feels they warrant it. He commented: "From a professional perspective, working in social media marketing, the way the club operate with influencers is world class. Arsenal, from a marketing perspective, are every inch the modern business. They monitor fan sentiment and they certainly keep track of the main blogs. They're a quick and easy snapshot of how the fans are feeling and they're also a useful PR tool for them. *Le Grove* certainly isn't in the inner circle of trusted bloggers, but it's pretty well known within digital circles that the club actively court certain bloggers with hospitality tickets as well as using the quite blatant carrot of hosting links to their content on the main home site." (*Arsenal.com* has a recommended reading page linking to media stories and blogs that are largely supportive, including *Goonerholic*, *A Cultured Left Foot* and *Arseblog*.)

Wood's own relationship with the club indicates how they are sufficiently broadminded not to ostracise their critics. He recalls: "The club invited me to meet Charles Allen [the head of marketing] to talk about their marketing plans, which interests me on a professional level. Ivan Gazidis was then available for an off-the-record Q&A. We were allowed to ask him what we liked. I think I was wheeled in to give credibility to the meeting, so it didn't look like an exercise in PR. I'd had a similar invitation to meet the medical team a couple of years prior to this. The club know I'm not out to shaft anyone, but they know

I won't sugar coat anything either, so if they get a positive story out of *Le Grove*, in the eyes of the club, it's worth more than one from more club friendly blogs."

At the other end of the spectrum are websites like *Untold Arsenal*, formed by Tony Atwood. Totally in the corner of the manager and the board, it even refers to the former as 'Lord Wenger' and the team's poor showings are often explained away as being down to biased refereeing. Modern achievements are measured against less successful eras, effectively reprising Conservative Prime Minister Harold Macmillan's 1957 slogan, "You've Never Had It So Good". Those who find fault with the manager and the club are referred to as AAA (Anti-Arsenal Arsenal). As *Le Grove* is representative of one group of supporters, so is *Untold Arsenal*. Rather like a religious or political conflict, there is little prospect of finding common ground unless, of course, the club returns to its glory days and everyone piles in behind the manager in the belief that he can turn back the clock.

The advance of social media has meant that online fans' opinions have largely rendered the fanzine movement that began in the late 1980s redundant. Only *The Gooner* is still sold at Arsenal home matches in any significant numbers, although its future as a magazine is uncertain. Its website (*www.onlinegooner.com*) offers a platform for more immediate views and reflects contributions from all sides of the Arsenal spectrum. However, the majority of submissions tend to reflect a gradual and increasing sense of disillusionment. So much so that when the title challenge of 2013/14 collapsed, there was a sense of resignation rather than anger in that it conformed to the pattern of past seasons.

With the passage of time, supporters now have the opportunity to be far more vociferous, influential and reach a wider audience than the days when a small collective such as the Arsenal Action Group lobbied for the removal of manager Terry Neill in 1983. As *Arseblogger* Andrew Mangan explains: "The world would be very boring without a range of opinion, and nothing divides people more than football. There are positive people, negative people, and people who can exist quite happily in the middle of those two extremes. To think that there's only one right way to support a club seems an arrogant idea to me, and most people have a range of things they think are going well and they think are going badly. Of course, there are people who go a bit too far at both ends of the spectrum (the ones who think the club can do nothing wrong and those who think it can do nothing right), but it's healthy that there are so many options out there."

It is in the interest of the club to keep tabs on everything that moves and shakes in the Arsenal world, which BSM's Kelvin Meadows confirms: "We know that what we say and do is being closely observed and our friends at the club do give us feedback on how our activities are being discussed." And Peter Wood concurs: "I think large organisations are sensitive to influencers who write about them every day. I don't think I shape events at the club, but I might make them think about things more than they would otherwise. As a fan who has access to lots of people who share things about the club, I might be able to put things on the agenda of the mainstream media." All the more reason for Arsenal to maintain a constructive engagement with the supporters' groups and opinion formers, which would be tried and tested as the denouement of 2013/14 approached.

This will require the directors to be even more open-minded. Prepared to work with the supporters when they needed them – to elicit support for the planning of the stadium and to learn the special culture of the club – the administrators soon felt comfortable that they knew what they were doing. Thus, with all three revenue streams – broadcast, commercial and matchday – continuing to thrive and deliver annual profits (£7 million in 2013), the supporters' groups have been moved to the margins. Certainly the dialogue continues, if only for the club to keep tabs on what is going on outside the walls of the boardroom and the executive suites, but there is no pressing need to bring any representative of a supporters' group into the inner sanctum. "A supporter on the board?" David Dein was fond of asking rhetorically. "What do you think we [the directors] are then?"

But the board is polarised between loyal, long-time serving septuagenarians, who are probably not in touch with the evolutionary development of technology, and Stan Kroenke and his son, Josh, who view their club with an American eye. With no compulsion to continue a dialogue with the fans, the impression is given that, like many American entrepreneurs, the Kroenkes will only start to worry, not if they see empty seats in the stadium, but if they represent unsold season tickets or corporate boxes.

As 2013/2014 moved towards its conclusion, with the quest for the title stuttering and even qualification for the Champions League hanging in the balance, the mood amongst the supporters could be described as discontented, if not in open revolt. Failure to land silverware for yet another year (especially as the largely favourable FA Cup draw unfolded round by round), and with millions of pounds sitting in the bank, then this mood would most likely change. Such a turn of events would test the relationship between the club and its supporters to the limit.

Chapter 11

Decline and Fall... and a Silver Lining

Arsène Wenger described the trio of disasters at the Etihad, Anfield and Stamford Bridge as "accidents." His description was accurate only in so far as the manner in which he approached those trials of strength – they were "accidents waiting to happen." After the third of these debacles, his team appeared to be suffering from post-traumatic stress disorder when they faced Swansea at home just three days after the Chelsea embarrassment. The positive attitude, *savior faire* and no little skill which had taken Arsenal to the top of the table and enabled them to retain the number one position from September to February was conspicuous by its absence. The knack of subjugating the lesser teams had apparently been mislaid and in its place an old habit had returned, namely the inability to preserve a lead. Certainly the 90th-minute equaliser Arsenal conceded in the 2-2 draw was an unfortunate own goal, but it occurred as a consequence of trying to score a third rather than concentrating on not conceding a second. Where had the solid defensive mindset of the previous season's run-in, when leads were protected in tight matches as if the players' lives depended on it, disappeared to?

With only two victories from the seven games since beating Crystal Palace 2-0 in the first week of February, a repeat of the 2012/13 face-saving run that salvaged fourth place was starting to look like an optimistic long shot. Arsenal had already descended to fourth spot and an in-form Everton side in fifth were closing fast. As a first step, an injection of confidence was required, but Manchester City were not the ideal visitors for such a task.

Once again the loss of possession in the midfield proved critical as the mercurial David Silva attacked the Arsenal back four with pace and, after laying the ball off to Dzeko, whose shot hit the post, followed up and deftly tapped in the rebound. One nil down at the break, but for the first time in a while Arsenal responded with commitment, made the most of their possession and equalised with a rare Flamini goal. The crowd left the stadium in a much better frame of mind than they had after the Swansea game earlier in the week, even if the end result was the same and two precious points had been dropped at home. Arsenal were now in fourth place and next up was Everton, their direct challenger for the last Champions League spot.

Once renowned as the most innovative of coaches, at Goodison Park Arsène Wenger was again on the receiving end of a lesson from a much younger man, Roberto Martinez, whose simple tactical plan he was unable to withstand. By switching Romelu Lukaku from his usual central position to wide on the right and filling the vacant space with an attacking midfielder (just as Brendan Rodgers had done with Luis Suarez and Philippe Coutinho at Anfield), Martinez exposed the Arsenal left flank and unsettled their entire defence. Perhaps Everton's task was eased by Wenger's selection of both Podolski and Cazorla on the wings, as neither was adept at providing protection for the full-backs. If the premeditated switch caught Wenger out, he certainly should not have been unaware of Leighton Baines' methods, which had made him the first-choice England full-back, or the similar offensive attributes of Seamus Coleman on the other flank, and raised the question of exactly how much thought the Arsenal manager had given to containing one of Everton's main attacking ploys. A typical marauding run by Baines led to the first goal, whilst Lukaku scored the second (surprise surprise) by cutting in from the right to shoot on his favoured left foot. The common denominator for this goal and the subsequent third was yet again the cheap squandering of possession. The 3-0 loss meant that Arsenal had taken five points from their last six matches, whilst Everton, with all the momentum and form of six wins in a row, were now a point behind Arsenal with a game in hand and well placed to grab the final Champions League place. Four visits to the homes of Manchester City, Liverpool, Chelsea and now Everton had seen Arsenal concede 20 goals, half their total for the 33 matches played. Arsène Wenger now had less than a week to restore some lost pride and self-belief.

The last time Arsenal emerged victorious from a penalty shoot-out in the FA Cup was against Manchester United in the 2005 final. After a tepid display, Arsenal became the undeserved holders of the FA Cup on that day. At least on Saturday 12th April 2014 against Wigan from the Championship, albeit the reigning cup holders who astonishingly had seen off Manchester City to reach the semi-final, Arsenal deserved to come out on top; 4-2 on penalties after extra time could not separate the teams at one goal apiece. The fact that Wigan's limited containment tactics were sufficiently successful to take the contest to penalties was due to the poverty of Arsenal's offensive manoeuvres. After the Premiership side had wasted a number of opportunities, Wigan took the lead from a second-half penalty. Arsenal still had time to rectify matters and Wenger switched to a more attacking 4-4-2 system, replacing Podolski with Giroud. The substitution was greeted with a chorus of boos directed specifically at the manager for removing the German international rather than Yaya Sanogo, who had once again tried the supporters' patience – four starts and six substitute appearances, though most were of only a few minutes' duration, had yet to see him register or even threaten a debut goal.

Despite creating some good chances – Sanogo almost broke his duck by hitting a post – the relief amongst the Arsenal supporters was palpable when Mertesacker equalised with only ten minutes remaining. There was still time for Oxlade-Chamberlain to rattle the woodwork in extra time, but there was no further addition to the score. And so to penalties; Arsenal were simply more clinical than Wigan, with a 100 per cent conversion rate, and emerged as the victors. They were the better of two average teams and as such deserved to triumph. On one level, the performance was not as important as reaching the final itself, but on another it was indicative of a deep-rooted disquiet as a thin squad was made to struggle by a team over 20 places below them in the league hierarchy.

So, as in the past couple of seasons, April was reached with Arsenal facing the necessity to fight off a challenge for fourth place in the Premier League after spending most of the time – 21 weeks – looking down on the rest of the table. Any sense of complacency at reaching the FA Cup final was wiped away when, three days later at the Emirates, they fell behind against West Ham. Then with an excellent riposte to the manager for his substitution in the semi-final, two goals from Podolski and one from Giroud returned the team to winning ways for the first time since beating Tottenham one month earlier. Five days later and another win was recorded as Hull City, their cup final opponents, were brushed aside 3-0 at their own place.

After three long months off duty, Aaron Ramsey had returned to action as a substitute in the visit to Everton, and then played the majority of the two hours it took to dismiss Wigan before being substituted with only eight minutes of extra time remaining. He made another reappearance from the bench against West Ham three days after the Wembley semi-final and was back in the starting line-up at Hull. Significantly, he featured prominently in all three Arsenal goals at the KC Stadium, one of which he claimed for himself whilst the other two belonged to Podolski. Ramsey's input underlined just how much his drive and pace had been missed along with that of Walcott. At least now with Ramsey's return, Arsenal could look forward with a degree of optimism to their last three games. Moreover, with Everton dropping points away to Southampton, two more home victories would see them reserve their seats for yet another ride on the Champions League gravy train, subject to progressing from the August qualifying round against unseeded opponents. The first of these, a 3-0 win against Newcastle, although not guaranteeing a seat, ensured that only a remarkable sequence of results would now be needed to keep them off the train. Once again Aaron Ramsey, who was easing himself back into top form just in time for the cup final, reaffirmed his inestimable value. Just as encouraging was Mesut Ozil's passable impression of Dennis Bergkamp, which had not been seen for some time. The German international did not appear to be particularly active, but he scored one goal and provided an excellent cross for Giroud to mark another after a rare set piece conversion by Koscielny had got the scoreline moving.

With fourth place now signed and sealed, after Everton's loss to Manchester City the day before, a lazy sunny Sunday afternoon stroll awaited the Gunners in their last home match of the season against West Bromwich Albion. Save a series of freakish results at the bottom of the table, for West Brom, like their hosts, nothing was at stake beyond the £1.2 million for every place in the final league table. Another set piece conversion by Giroud illustrated just how effective a chip into the box for the big men eager to participate in the action was as a variation to the overused short passing and measured build-up.

Arsenal signed off their 2013/14 campaign with an academic encounter against Norwich, who were already doomed unless their opponents could equal the combined generosity of previous capitulations against Manchester City, Liverpool and Chelsea and provide the 17 goals they needed to avoid relegation. There were cameo appearances from the long-indisposed Wilshere and Diaby, and just as rare as seeing the French international in a red and white shirt was a Carl Jenkinson goal (his first for the club) after Ramsey had opened the scoring with a sublime volley.

The 2-0 result took Arsenal to 79 points. As this total followed on from 68 in 2010/11, 70 in 2011/12 and 73 in 2012/13, Arsène Wenger argued that he was on a gradual upward curve of improvement: "Unfortunately, it's the first time in the Premier League that you finish fourth with 79 points and it was very tight," he remarked. "We can be frustrated. We have won 11 games away from home, I think it's the best in the league and it was our 17th clean sheet – that is remarkable as well." However, the muted celebration for fourth place was in stark contrast to the relief and joy of the previous year's achievement, which was explained by the *Online Gooner*: "And the reason is because this time around, Arsenal fell away from first place whereas a year ago, they rose from below the top four. Football is about hope. When there is no chance of first place, falling well short of it does not hurt so much. But to have been in the position Arsenal were in at the beginning of February has led to severe disappointment, not least because of the nature of the team's capitulation in the matches that derailed their challenge."

But there was still, thankfully, one more game to play before the season could officially be consigned to history. On 17th May Arsène Wenger would lead out his team on the Wembley pitch in the FA Cup final against Hull City. Coincidentally, the final game of 2013/14 season would also be the last one of Wenger's contract. And with his new one yet to be signed, Arsenal supporters could be forgiven for wondering whether their first FA Cup final in nearly a decade would presage a new glorious chapter or be the anti-climatic final page in the manager's love story with the club.

Chapter 12

The Cup Runneth Over

"You can't be complacent. I remember in '88 against Luton in the League Cup final. With ten minutes to go and it was the first time I was captain [in a final], I looked across at the Royal Box and I saw the trophy and I thought we were 2-1 up, in ten minutes I am going to walk up those steps and lift that trophy for the Arsenal. And then bang, bang, bang, we lost 3-2 and I thought to myself I am never going to do that again. They [the current Arsenal squad] had a warning against Birmingham [in the League Cup in 2011] you can't take anything for granted. You have to remember those days how you felt after that game when you lost. You go out there and it [should be] the only game that matters, the only game that matters. You have to play like it's your last game. That's what I will be telling them all. Whether anybody is telling them that I don't know, but [if I was playing] I would certainly be in that dressing room, pacing up and down saying, "Come on guys, this is it." Tony Adams[9]

---

[9] Taken from an interview with talkSPORT Radio in May 2014.

Well it's all over now. Despite tempting fate by making arrangements for the victory parade and the immature tweet from Yaya Sanogo – "Last tweet b4 history, who would guess we wld be in this position 1 month ago? So Jose how much trophy did you get this year?" – Arsenal made it over the finishing line.

Nine long years since they last had their hands on a trophy. Yet it was a close run thing. As in their previous key encounters away from home, Arsenal started far too slowly in the FA Cup final against Hull City. They had saved their semi-final against Wigan eight minutes from time and now in the final they were two goals down after eight minutes, and if Kieran Gibbs had not headed off the line five minutes later to prevent Hull City from taking a three-goal lead, it is unlikely that the Gunners could have turned the tables. Just as in the semi-final, if they had been facing a stronger team there might have been no way back, despite the positive response to their initial trepidation: "We were a bit timid from the start in the semi-final," Per Mertesacker recalled. "When they [Wigan] scored we were a bit frightened, but we came back. We [now] know that anything can happen, especially in a final. I think we are aware that if something happens we will not collapse."

So it was that Gibbs' last-ditch clearance was the turning point. Shaken and stirred, the thousands of Arsenal fans had rocked the stadium with cacophonous support and the team responded. Three minutes later and Cazorla, fouled just outside the penalty area, exacted his revenge with a sublimely struck free kick from 25 yards. At 2-1 down Arsenal now had a foothold in the game, which assumed the pattern of play anticipated before kick-off; they pushed forward as a result of having the majority of possession, whilst Hull harried and hustled, awaiting a chance to counter-attack.

Perhaps recent Arsenal teams would have been disheartened by the rejection by the referee, Lee Probert, of two good claims for a penalty, but this bunch was made of sterner stuff and, as Mertesacker had forecast, pushed on, although with the movement in the final third lacking cohesion they offered no real danger to the Hull goal. All that changed in the 60th minute when Arsène Wenger went back to the future with a tactical 4-4-2 formation. He replaced Lukas Podolski with Sanogo, which gave the Hull defence two strikers to worry about and the Arsenal midfield two target men to get the ball quickly to before moving up in support to capitalise on their layoffs.

Now Arsenal started to create chances in and around the penalty area, but needed the incorrect award of a corner kick and a fortuitous subsequent ricochet to score. The ball dropped to Laurent Koscielny a few yards out, and he bravely stabbed it into the net in the 71st minute.

As the game moved into extra time the Arsenal manager upped the ante and went for victory. The fresh legs of Wilshere and Rosicky, who replaced Ozil and Cazorla, pushed Hull back and created space. Above all, Arsène Wenger wanted to avoid the hazardous necessity of spot-kicks so much that he took a calculated risk with his late substitutions. "I tried desperately not to go to penalties because I did not have many players on the pitch who were specialists at it. I tried to go for it before the end," he explained after the match. "Cazorla is a serious penalty taker and that's why I was hesitant [to take him off]. I was worried by the decision I was making because I had two strikers on the pitch. Jack [Wilshere] is not a penalty taker, Rosicky is not a penalty taker. Giroud had cramp so it was difficult."

With only 11 minutes of extra time remaining, Aaron Ramsey seized on a sublime Giroud backheel to score the deserved winner. The grand finale was most appropriate as Ramsey, Arsenal's player of the season, and Cazorla, Arsenal's player of the match, had worked tirelessly to push the team forward. So in this instance, fortune favoured the brave. "It paid off, but we had a horrible feeling for a long time in the game and in the end it was a relief. The job is how it finishes, all the rest nobody cares," Wenger said. Indeed. The last Arsenal trophy that was constantly being harked back to was won via a penalty shoot-out. That this time the *coup de grâce* was delivered without the need to resort to penalties spared many frazzled nerves. However, had it been necessary to do so, the celebrations would have been just as joyous.

Prior to the FA Cup final, the Champions League spot having been secured, there appeared to be no obstacle for Wenger to sign his contract. Yet he had not done so. Perhaps, even if Arsenal had lost he would have eventually signed on and stayed. Conspiracy theorists might have argued that the news that he had been offered a two-year deal only emerged when Arsenal were threatened for fourth place by Everton and there was a distinct possibility of the season ending in hubris. Further, the short length of the deal – two years was unusual in the volatile world of the Premier League – would not antagonise the anti-Wenger faction, who could foresee that, if matters deteriorated, the board could always call a premature halt without incurring too weighty a financial penalty. The day after the final, Wenger's employers announced that they expected him to sign a three-year deal, thought to be worth around £24 million, thereby bringing to an end the protracted contractual standoff with no one prepared to explain why it had been allowed to run its course beyond the final match.

During the media conferences in the run-up to the final, Wenger was not only irritated by questions about his contract; he also took exception to the constant probing about the reasons for the lack of a trophy. "Look, it has become a way to think for everybody like that," he said. "If you look at the overall consistency, nobody has finished in the Champions League for 18 years [in a row]. Nobody. But it is true that because we are used to winning every year and suddenly you don't win, it becomes a way of thinking [for his critics]. But you could go to some other clubs [and ask], 'Why did you not win the championship for twenty years?' Nobody asks them the question. Having said that, of course, we want to win every year, but it is difficult." For all the talk of profits and entertaining and enticing play, in his innermost being Wenger knew that nothing would be more acceptable to anyone connected with the club than a trophy. "It matters for your fans," he said. "It matters for us. It's a concrete sign that you win. I love to win. Your fans love you to win. Your fans will be happy when you win trophies." When asked if there is something missing if you don't win trophies, Wenger replied, "Yes, that's true."

At the end of his new three-year deal, Arsène Wenger will be 67 and will have completed a total of 20 years in the job. His past trophy wins have ushered in a new era of repeated success. It is unlikely, though, that this one will do likewise as the competition has grown, become more fierce and will get tougher still in the years to come. Nevertheless, what the FA Cup win of 2014 has provided are many positives, not least of which was the delight that the many thousands of his admirers took in seeing the manager skipping around like a teenager. He celebrated with such gusto that the rare display of uninhibited extrovertism brought to mind that, if Arsenal had lost, the disillusionment might just have been too great for him to bear and he would have had to walk away. So distressing were the league upsets against his main rivals – "I am a bad loser. I have heard that and I have read that. I think even my wife would agree with you that I am a bad loser," he told a friend – and the wounds were all the deeper for his belief that these failures were down to him, his faults, his mistakes that caused them to be inflicted, that the victory was relished so much. As he had admitted on many occasions, "I love to win."

Wenger's boys now knew what it was like to share the winning sensation (which their female counterparts, Arsenal Ladies, had long been accustomed to, their latest trophy being the FA Women's Cup of 2014), so the pressure of abject performances and near misses could recede into the background. And at least they could now reflect dispassionately that being top of the Premier League but failing to remain so was a better situation than having to play desperate catch-up. Back in January, if the fans had been asked to settle for the FA Cup and fourth place many would have felt let down, but in May it brought only happiness. The Emirates Stadium now has a glorious present, the first trophy captured since the move from Highbury, and the new home is now no longer out of step with the recollections of the historic past which were enacted elsewhere, even if it was only a quarter of a mile down the road. As Tony Adams told Carl Jenkinson and Kieran Gibbs before the final: "In '87 when I had been at the club four years and we hadn't won anything, we had a great bunch of guys coming through – Rocky [David Rocastle], Michael Thomas, Paul Merson, Martin Keown, Niall Quinn and I could go on – and we won that League Cup against Liverpool, that kind of sent us on our way. It was a pivotal moment in my career and I shared it with the [two] guys and said, "look, win it for god's sake."'

Above all there was a solid platform for the manager to move forward despite Lukasz Fabianski (who Wenger had kept faith with as his cup goalkeeper) and Bacary Sagna coming to the end of their contracts and likely to leave. Wenger was prepared to offer the 31-year-old right-back a three-year deal and a substantial rise in wages, but could not hide the fact that the contract of yet another top player, the most experienced in the current squad, had been allowed to run down to leave him in a weak negotiating position in an endeavour to retain his services. (Fabianski subsequently joined Swansea City and Sagna Manchester City).

A bad start to the new term. However, unlike past seasons the bulk of the first-team squad were on long-term contracts, while others like Nicklas Bendtner and Park Chu-Young, who had not earned their keep, could be finally jettisoned with the concomitant reduction in the wage bill. But it remains to be seen if the fans' opening day instruction to spend will be heeded in the next transfer window. With commercial revenues on a continuous upward curve, the media suggested that the manager was likely to be entrusted with a transfer budget of £100 million, with a replacement for Sagna to be added to the long overdue need for defensive cover at the back and in the midfield, together with two more striking options. There must be no repetition of last season's indolence.

But for the time being, all that speculation could be put on hold. Now was the moment for thousands of Arsenal fans to throng the streets of Islington to join in the victory parade, and for millions of others around the world to bask in the sheer pleasure that their team had won the FA Cup, the oldest and perhaps still the most authentic cup competition of them all.

Chapter 13

The Story Continues...

In the build-up to Arsène Wenger's 1,000th competitive match as Arsenal manager on 22nd March 2014, his long-term ally, David Dein, asked him, "What does that mean to you?" His friend replied, "1,000 sleepless nights." There were undoubtedly a few more in the aftermath of the 6-0 spanking at Stamford Bridge that marked the milestone in the worst possible way.

Although there had been sporadic upsets of a similar nature in the past, this one, encompassing as it did the results at the Etihad and Anfield within less than four months, was a cutting indictment. David Dein knew that the manager would be ruminating over the reverse and that any possible convivial dinner date at a local Totteridge restaurant for themselves and their spouses, which was the frequent postscript to a satisfactory result earlier in the day, was completely out of the question. Wenger would be beating himself up until the wee small hours in his secluded, gated mansion. A sympathetic phone call would have to suffice.

The Arsenal boss would also be able to draw on similar support from acolytes such as Thierry Henry, who, when crisis struck, would habitually warn Wenger's critics: "Be careful what you wish for because you never know who is going to come after. How's it going to be? So you have to be careful what you are going to do next."

The observation, though, was just as apposite for the man himself. Where would he go? What would he do if he called an end to his life's work? Maybe the close-but-no-cigar finishes of the last few seasons had devalued David Dein's claim that "Arsène could walk into any top club in the world", but there were still presidents waiting to welcome him with open arms. Despite taking Monaco to the runners-up position and a Champions League spot in their first season back in the French top division, Claudio Ranieri had been dismissed in May 2014 and a spectacular offer to replace him was reportedly on its way to north London. And the French Champions, Paris St Germain, always had a soft spot for Wenger. Moreover, his wife, Annie, had said the family would ultimately return to France. Maybe now would be a good opportunity. However, the respective billionaire Russian and Qatari owners of the two French clubs would want to do his shopping for him and might even insist on the appointment of a sporting director to 'help' him. "It's not his style,'" said Dein conclusively.

"Arsène seriously thought about taking a break," revealed Dein in Lisbon on the day of the Champions League final, confirming that the opprobrium from both the media and the fans Wenger had received in the previous months had made him think long and hard about whether he felt like continuing. For the moment, staying put certainly suits the Wengers, if for no other reason than their daughter Lea embarked on a university course in September 2014.

For a football obsessive who is also stubborn and set in his ways, Arsène Wenger was never going to get a better job than the one he already had. He is the main man at one of the top ten wealthiest football clubs in the world, whose employers, unlike those at Real Madrid, Barcelona, Bayern Munich, Manchester United, Paris St Germain, Manchester City and Chelsea (the clubs above Arsenal in the pecking order), together with Juventus and AC Milan who complete the list, do not expect him to obtain the league title or the Champions League trophy. Seemingly there is no one who cares to challenge him and hold him to account for such obvious errors over the course of the previous season, such as his tactics against Chelsea, the lack of transfer activity (both in the summer of 2013 and in January 2014) and the way he prepared his teams for the crucial confrontations.

As Wenger once asked rhetorically, "Who motivates the motivator?" the absence of David Dein by his side has grown increasingly conspicuous as the seasons have gone by. Never one to challenge his mentor when one trophy followed another, nevertheless it was Dein who first saw the writing on the wall as he noted Chelsea's new *modus vivendi* – "Roman Abramovich has parked his tanks on our lawn and is firing fifty pound notes at us" – which eventually convinced him that money and lots of it would be the only way to keep his club competitive.

When the reputation of Arsenal was at stake, Dein tended to act first, often off his own bat, and think about the repercussions afterwards. Hence his premature wooing of Stan Kroenke, with the ironic consequence that his overtures paved the way for the American entrepreneur to assume control whilst he, having shown Arsenal the money, was shown the door. Dein's ambition was Arsenal-centric first and foremost. A salient example occurred in 1999. In a fourth-round FA Cup tie, when Marc Overmars scored after Sheffield United had stopped play expecting the ball to be returned to them (after they had put it out of play so an Arsenal injury could be dealt with) and the final whistle was blown with Arsenal victorious, Dein was out of his director's seat at Highbury quicker than Usain Bolt. Intercepting Wenger before he reached the dressing room, and uninterested in whether or not the manager felt the result should stand, Dein presented him with a *fait accompli* that it was not in the Arsenal book of ethics to win in the way they had. Accordingly the cup tie was replayed and Wenger received plaudits from the media for his sporting gesture and even the Fair Play Award from UEFA, while Dein resumed his usual spot out of the limelight, content that Arsenal's reputation was not only unsullied but enhanced. Once again, Dein had acted in the manner he felt was in Arsenal's best interests, and if he was around now one could be fairly sure that every last penny of the transfer budget would be spent in order to fulfill the message he used to see emblazoned on his forehead every morning when he looked in the mirror to shave before going to the office: "Get a winning team."

Even without his friend and confident, on the margins of the manager's responsibilities there were positive signs in 2014 of a more conciliatory attitude, namely the acceptance of new brooms in the youth set-up, a readiness to try and get to the bottom of the appalling injury record and the eventual acquisition of a world-class player at a world-class price. Perhaps CEO Ivan Gazidis can take another bigger step forward, push the door a bit further open and help to instigate some long overdue changes in the playing strategy.

Looking around at his rivals' prospects in the summer of 2013 should have encouraged Wenger to let boldness be his friend. United, City and Chelsea all had new managers to bed in and it was always likely that Tottenham, being Tottenham, would soon join them in what would prove to be a season of transition for all of them. Likewise for Liverpool, at least at the start with Luis Suarez absent for the first couple of months and his employers wondering what frame of mind he would be in on his return. Moreover, the increased revenue streams, particularly broadcast and commercial, no longer made it imperative for Arsène to sell his best players in order to turn a profit. Instead, for the first time he bought a ready-made star of his own, but only as a last-minute afterthought, which prevented any pre-planning that could have made the most value from the purchase. To maximise the full range of Mesut Ozil's supreme passing ability, pace up front was obligatory so the midfielder could play the ball into space as well as to feet. Even after Walcott's indisposition underlined the missed opportunity, the chance to rectify the problem in the January transfer window was spurned. If he couldn't obtain the specific person he wanted, Wenger tended to settle for what he had rather than go for an alternative; the player might still be better than those in his first-team squad, but in his mind they always carried the stigma of being second best. And as late as March 2014, according to David Dein, Wenger still subscribed to the same thought: "It's not not wanting to spend money, it's identifying the talent which is the key point," Dein said. "He will only buy a player if he really thinks it's a player who will improve the squad, who is better than what we've got at the moment, without stultifying and frustrating the development of a young player. There's no point in putting talent on top of talent. He won't do that because he doesn't want to frustrate the ambitions of a younger player."

So when the Suarez trail petered out, so did his interest in strikers *per se*. Yet Loic Remy and Wilfred Bony, both of whom subsequently ended the season with a superior strike rate to Olivier Giroud, were available, and, as late as January, Hull City saved their Premier League place with the purchases of Nikica Jelavic and Shane Long, who, if they had not been cup-tied, might have won the FA Cup for their side. But Wenger stubbornly persisted in putting all his eggs in Giroud's basket. In mid-November, he said: "Giroud has good stamina, strong body and great hunger for the game. I don't see any sign of fatigue." By January it was obvious that the manager had not been to SpecSavers and had no intention of doing so, and thus had no alternative but to continue to flog a horse which, if it had not quite expired, was on its last legs.

Even with the players at his disposal, it is debatable whether the manager's tactics brought out the best in them. When the media suggested that maybe he did not pay enough attention to the opposition, Wenger bridled and rejected the idea out of hand. However, the facts tell a different story. Sure, the quality of Arsenal's passing can subdue lesser teams, even when they know what is in store for them, but not the better ones who, through the calibre of their personnel, can counter Arsenal's predictable plans. With Walcott unavailable, the team had no pace to call on and they had little power to begin with, so Chelsea, Liverpool and Manchester City, and even Everton and Southampton on their day, found that all they had to do to discombobulate the Gunners was to push up, pressurise the midfield so they relinquished possession and then strike quickly through the heart of the defence.

As he told a friend at the Football Writers' Dinner, two days before the FA Cup final, and Radio 5 Live listeners the day after (who did not have the benefit of his animated gestures to punctuate his points), Frank McLintock stated that: "Arsenal need a change of tactics, but I don't think Arsène will change at all. When you look at the first two goals against Chelsea, the two full-backs were 30 yards ahead of the two centre halves and the centre halves were 30 yards apart [from each other]. If we [his Arsenal double-winning side of 1971] were playing, what usually happened for the first 20 minutes away from home against a [top] team, you try and shut up shop. You have all the back four in place and your central midfield player [as well]. Pat Rice would have been ten yards to my right. Peter Simpson would have been ten yards to my left. Bob McNab would be within 20 yards [of me], and Peter Storey would be sitting in front of us, so when the opposition looked up there would be no space to be seen. But when you play against Arsenal [in 2013/14] they are bombing forward. If you're going to play like that, as Barcelona do, you've got to pressurise the ball as soon as you lose it. But Arsenal don't do that. They try and play the Barcelona way, but when they have not got the ball they are absolutely useless. They are five to eight yards off the opposition and you can't play like that. You are too wide open and it proved itself in at least three matches [Liverpool, Chelsea and Everton – and also Manchester City] and yesterday [against Hull City] as well."

Dumbfounded, like a boxer on the ropes unable to avoid the punishment that was being dished out to him, Arsène Wenger had just rolled with the punches. There was no attempt at the unexpected and no unforeseen surprise packet, and that's why the switch to 4-4-2 in the cup final was such an eye opener until you understood the manager's fear of penalties. And the fact that the chop and change worked was really in spite of Yaya Sanogo's limited abilities. (If Wenger had the luxury of choice and a better striker to call on, the game might well have been over in his favour within 90 minutes.) An exchange with a friend in 2004 puts some perspective on Wenger's lack of tactical acumen and his reluctance to use substitutes to modify his pattern of play.

'You know people say you don't see things because you're down on the pitch – you can't see, can you?"

"Yes, it's true. I can't see. But what is [also] true – because I have this reputation now, I used it once or twice not to come out against my players but now even when I'm honest, people don't believe me. Because it's true, you're in a bad position to see everything."

"Because you stand where you do when you watch a game, maybe you can't make the best substitutions because you can't see the flow of the game. Why do you feel that you should be there?"

"Because I started my job in there [as an assistant coach] and I feel I have good vision. I am used to it. I don't like the physical separation from the team."

"But am I right when I say that might be why sometimes the substitutions aren't right – because you can't see the strategic overall pattern?"

[Irritated] "No. It's not true – that's your opinion. And it's not true your opinion is right. They are not your substitutions. When you speak about substitutions, it's just an opinion. I can find you 50,000 different opinions in the crowd, but people ignore many things I know when you look at substitutions."

"Such as?"

"Such as, I know that this guy will die after an hour physically. Because I know in the last three games after an hour his high intensity dropped 30 per cent or 40 per cent and he will not be capable of keeping going."

So there you have it. And succeeding seasons have not disproved the notion that Wenger's substitutions are made for physical rather than tactical reasons. No surprise then that none were made in order to get to half time without incurring further damage after the opening shellackings at Anfield and Stamford Bridge (raising the question of Steve Bould's impotence once the referee blows his whistle). Wenger played these games to win from the start, for his team to impose their tempo on their opponents, and persisted with the tactic even after the early setbacks. Such routs leave an indelible wound. They undermine the very fundamentals of a winning mentality – heart, an innate and deep-seated self-belief, a strong work ethic and the willingness to go to the wire with comrades in a common cause. These are the basic attributes that were found wanting whenever Arsenal came out to play against the big boys, yet when present they can upset the odds, as exemplified by the displays of Atletico Madrid in 2013/14.

Whilst the drama of the FA Cup final was unfolding, Atletico Madrid were drawing their last *La Liga* fixture at Barcelona to take the title from their hosts. A week later, they came within two minutes of upsetting Real Madrid to wrap up the Champions League, before extra time finally took its toll. Moreover, for the most important game in their history, their two key men made a negligible contribution: Diego Costa had to be withdrawn after only nine minutes, while Arda Turan never even entered the field of play. The financial disparity between Atletico and the habitual winners of the Spanish title, Barcelona and Real, is far greater – the income attained by Atletico is only a quarter of the astronomical sums that Real Madrid and Barcelona each earn – than the gap that divides Arsenal and the three wealthier clubs in England – Manchester United, Chelsea and Manchester City.

Furthermore, Atletico's squad cost a mere £30 million to assemble as opposed to the £330 million of Real, whilst their wage bill was less than that of relegated Fulham. Diego Costa was just the latest in a production line of star strikers – following Fernando Torres, Sergio Aguero and Radamel Falcao – whose multi-million pound transfers have kept the club afloat.

Before reaching the summit with the 2014 *La Liga* title, Atletico had gradually made their way to the higher levels of both the continental and domestic game. The Europa League was secured in 2012 and the *Copa del Rey* in 2013. Neither trophy, like the FA Cup, would have substantially aided their bank balance, but undoubtedly engendered a winning mentality. Defeating Champions League winners Chelsea in the 2012 European Super Cup would have done no harm to their self-belief either. With the quality of leadership and personal chemistry of the coach, Diego Simeone, for whom veteran Portuguese international Tiago Mendes stated he would "jump off a bridge" for, instilling a work ethic that made light of having to sell their stars, Atletico's roll of honour was a demonstration of what could be achieved with the right philosophy and how an initial cup success may provide a platform to go on and reach for the stars.

When he first arrived in England in 1996, Arsène Wenger was rightfully hailed as a revolutionary. The innovations he wrought in coaching, training and match preparation, including exercise and diet, though not uncommon on the continent, were unknown in England. He reaped the rewards of an *avant garde* modernist. An example to be emulated, Wenger opened the eyes of other managers, and their voyages of discovery eventually led to new and better disciplines and a propensity for financial risk-taking, which left the original revolutionary mired in his now outmoded *modus operandi*.

"Would you say," Wenger was asked in 2008, "that you're constantly evolving, changing things off the field in terms of exercise, nutrition, preparation?"

"Yes, in terms of the evolution of the game as well. On that front, I like to move on, always."

"Can you give me an example of something you've changed and you've been pleased with the result?"

"Not really because we'd have to go deep into exercises. What I mean is I fight against the fact that when you are successful you keep doing the same thing because that's preparing the failure of tomorrow. And it's a temptation that is very strong. For example, when I arrived here [in England] in the way that we built the team, we had a more physical impact team. Now we have a more mobile and technical team."

"You think that's the future? A more mobile team?"

"It's what I like. To express this on the field and go to the end of my thinking was important to me to see if it works."

Maybe Wenger has persisted for too long in prioritising mobility. His tenure as manager has been a case of feast and famine. His first 500 matches witnessed seven major honours (and two further final appearances), whereas the following 500 saw only three lost finals (and two of those were in the League Cup). The successful 2014 final was his 1,010th game. Whether the future will prove more fruitful than the first few years at the Emirates will be dependent on Wenger's willingness to move forward with wholesale changes.

The first step in the catch-up process in order to compete at the very highest level is giving the playing squad a root and branch overhaul, and the manager must show that he has consigned to history any reservations that he might have had with regard to lavish spending

"If money was no object," Wenger was asked in 2004, "and you could buy anyone to improve the team, who would you buy?"

"At the moment, nobody."

"You wouldn't buy Zidane?"

"Well, I wouldn't buy Zidane at the moment because... he's too old. And that's just lost money."

"But if I gave you unlimited money, you still wouldn't buy a world-class defender, would you?"

"No. Because you would be amazed how good we are with our young players."

The same parsimony was apparent when, some years later, Danny Fiszman asked him casually over dinner, "Arsène, what would you do if I gave you £100 million?" And Wenger replied, "I would give it back to you."

The lack of cash excuse is passé. All the precepts, such as sports science and training which hitherto gave him a competitive edge, no longer measure up when you are faced with world-class players and you do not have any of your own to respond with. Arsène has to face the fact that you can not win the Premier League or the Champions League without great players. And of course, they will not come cheap.

Where is the lightning-quick striker? And the midfield powerhouse? Where are the type of players who made his reputation? Where is the pace and power? The chronic problem of too many injuries will not be resolved overnight, so the squad needs much greater depth to ensure there is always a strong bench to call on. "I think that they will be in the top four next season [2014/15] even with the squad they have got," said George Graham. "But if they want to move on they've got to get more quality on the pitch." However, if you are not evolving you are stagnating and it is difficult to see a man in his mid-60s embracing a new revolution with a financial impetus, particularly one that is not of his own making or his predilection. Moreover the indications are that Wenger has yet to face up to the full implications of what might be involved. "The truth is, the most suitable system," Wenger says, "is that which suits the players you have, and the style of play has to reflect the personality of the manager, because you can't go against your own beliefs… You can question our system, but when we win a big game, everybody forgets about it. When you lose it, everybody says you should have played differently."

Perhaps Wenger should look at an even older man, a venerable OAP, who maintained an astonishing run of success. In Arsenal's first seven seasons at the Emirates, Sir Alex Ferguson's Manchester United reached three Champions League finals (winning one), took home the Premier League title five times and the League Cup twice. Though like Wenger he was omnipotent, unlike Wenger he was not omnipresent. He delegated training to trusted assistants, refreshed the quality personnel often enough to prevent complacency and instil new ideas, and, importantly, left the paramount role in transfer and wage negotiations to David Gill.

Ivan Gazidis, Gill's opposite number at Arsenal, does not have the same freedom to manoeuvre. Peter Wood of *Le Grove* recalled a revealing rendezvous with the CEO: "Ivan is a fiery character. He was very passionate and protective over his staff and the efforts that go on behind the scenes. The meeting for me felt like he was trying to communicate to the fans that he's doing all he can to give the manager the funds he needs. He made the point that cash in the bank with a base rate of 0.5 per cent is worth nothing, especially considering player inflation. He also pushed the point time and time again that he has to trust the manager to make the right decisions. He hears the criticism, he clearly reads it and it bothers him people think he and his team don't know what they're doing. For me, what was clear is that he's caught between a rock and a hard place. He has a manager who is a legend in the fans' eyes despite consistent failure to address progressive stagnation. He has an owner who is in awe of his very own 'Billy Beane' [The General Manager of baseball's Oakland A's, whose innovatory use of the wealth of available data to aid acquisition, selection and tactics, achieved the sort of success that would be comparable to Southampton qualifying for the Champions League], so he's stymied. He can't enact any sort of vision until the manager leaves, despite clearly knowing the problems at the club on the playing side all sit with Arsène Wenger and his dated approach to modern-day management. For me the message was clear, the club know what's going on but there's nothing anyone can do unless Arsène makes the first move."

Late in 2012, Wenger said: "I feel responsible for the evolution of the club. When you've been here for 16 years, you're part of the history and the guy who is responsible for the values that the club wants to show in all aspects of daily life. For example, if a manager changes every two years and the players stay for ten years, the players will always have a greater influence. If a manager stays at a club for 15 years, he is a 'memory' of the club." The Arsenal board had offered Wenger the opportunity to prolong the memories and publicly stated as much on more than one occasion. Because of the financial stability he had brought, through a mixture of continuous Champions League representation and his prudent transfer operations, he was regarded as the safest pair of hands available. After finally, at the end of May 2014, putting pen to paper on a £24 million three-year deal that will extend his tenure in north London to 20 years, Wenger said: "I want to stay and to continue to develop the team and the club. We are entering a very exciting period. We have a strong squad, financial stability and huge support around the world. We are all determined to bring more success."

In the summer of 2013 Ivan Gazidis left no doubt that the club had the means to buy big and thus transferred the onus to do so onto the manager. Having eventually put a trophy in the cabinet, while a nice end in itself, the FA Cup would be best served as a stepping stone to move forward. The CEO can now legitimately suggest that his manager listen to his experts and be more tolerant of them, but that if they are found wanting then he is welcome to bring in better backroom staff. And that the only way forward is to spend, spend, spend (but not like Tottenham).